New Explorations for Instructional Leaders

BRIDGING THEORY AND PRACTICE

This international series reflects the latest cutting-edge theories and practices in school leadership. Uniquely, we include books that bridge the perennial divide between theory and practice. The series motto is framed after Kurt Lewin's famous statement, and we paraphrase that there is no sound theory without practice and no good practice that is not framed on some theory.

* * * * * * * * * *

Books already published in the Series:

Brown, K. (2011). *Preparing future leaders for social justice, equity, and excellence: Bridging theory and practice through a transformative andragogy* (1st ed.). Rowman & Littlefield.

Brown, K., & Shaked, H. (2018). *Preparing future leaders for social justice: Bridging theory and practice through a transformative andragogy* (2nd ed.). Rowman & Littlefield.

Glanz, J. (Ed.). (2021). *Crisis and pandemic leadership: Implications for meeting the needs of students, teachers, and parents.* Rowman & Littlefield.

Glanz, J. (2022). *Managing today's schools: New skills for school leaders in the 21st century.* Rowman & Littlefield.

Stader, D. (2012). *Leadership for a culture of school safety: Linking theory to practice.* Rowman & Littlefield.

Zepeda, S. J. (Ed.). (2008). *Real world supervision: Adapting theory to practice.* Rowman & Littlefield.

Zepeda, S. J. (Ed.). (2018). *The job-embedded nature of coaching: Lessons and insights for school leaders.* Rowman & Littlefield.

Zepeda, S. J. (Ed.). (2018). *Making learning job-embedded: Cases from the field of educational leadership.* Rowman & Littlefield.

New Explorations for Instructional Leaders

How Principals Can Promote Teaching and Learning Effectively

Haim Shaked

ROWMAN & LITTLEFIELD
Lanham • Boulder • New York • London

Published by Rowman & Littlefield
An imprint of The Rowman & Littlefield Publishing Group, Inc.
4501 Forbes Boulevard, Suite 200, Lanham, Maryland 20706
www.rowman.com

86-90 Paul Street, London EC2A 4NE, United Kingdom

Copyright © 2023 by Haim Shaked

All rights reserved. No part of this book may be reproduced in any form or by any electronic or mechanical means, including information storage and retrieval systems, without written permission from the publisher, except by a reviewer who may quote passages in a review.

British Library Cataloguing in Publication Information Available

Library of Congress Cataloging-in-Publication Data

Names: Shaked, Haim Yehuda, 1968- author.
Title: New explorations for instructional leaders : how principals can promote teaching and learning effectively / Haim Shaked.
Description: Lanham : Rowman & Littlefield, [2023] | Series: Bridging theory and practice | Includes bibliographical references and index. | Summary: "What supports the application of instructional leadership? What hinders it? When is it incompletely applied? Although some researchers have explored such questions, the available knowledge on the application of instructional leadership is meager. New Explorations for Instructional Leaders provides up-to-date answers to these important questions"— Provided by publisher.
Identifiers: LCCN 2022032217 (print) | LCCN 2022032218 (ebook) | ISBN 9781475868739 (cloth) | ISBN 9781475868746 (paperback) | ISBN 9781475868753 (epub)
Subjects: LCSH: School supervision. | Educational leadership. | Effective teaching. | Teacher-principal relationships.
Classification: LCC LB2806.4 .S4795 2023 (print) | LCC LB2806.4 (ebook) | DDC 371.2/011—dc23/eng/20220825
LC record available at https://lccn.loc.gov/2022032217
LC ebook record available at https://lccn.loc.gov/2022032218

Contents

List of Figures	vii
List of Tables	ix
Foreword	xi
Preface	xv
Acknowledgments	xxi
Series Editor's Introduction	xxiii
Introduction: What is Instructional Leadership?	xxix

PART I: ENABLERS OF INSTRUCTIONAL LEADERSHIP APPLICATION ... 1

Chapter 1: Knowledge Enabling Instructional Leadership Application ... 3

Chapter 2: Relationships Enabling Instructional Leadership Application ... 15

Chapter 3: Systems Thinking as an Enabler of Instructional Leadership Application ... 27

PART II: INHIBITORS OF INSTRUCTIONAL LEADERSHIP APPLICATION ... 43

Chapter 4: Perceptions Inhibiting Instructional Leadership Application ... 45

Chapter 5: Clan Culture as an Inhibitor of Instructional Leadership Application ... 55

Chapter 6: Low Power Distance as an Inhibitor of Instructional Leadership Application — 63

Chapter 7: Inhibitors of Instructional Leadership Application in Rural Education — 71

PART III: INCOMPLETE APPLICATION OF INSTRUCTIONAL LEADERSHIP — 81

Chapter 8: Principals' Incomplete Performance of Teacher Evaluation — 83

Chapter 9: Principals' Incomplete Assurance of Teachers' Job Suitability — 93

Chapter 10: Assistant Principals' Incomplete Application of Instructional Leadership — 105

PART IV: PARADOXICAL SOLUTIONS TO INSTRUCTIONAL LEADERSHIP APPLICATION — 115

Chapter 11: A Paradoxical Approach to Instructional Leadership Application — 117

Chapter 12: A Paradoxical Approach in Practice: Instructional Leadership Application and Boundary Management — 125

Epilogue: Answering the "So What?" Question — 137

Index — 141

About the Author — 151

List of Figures

Figure 1: The Construct of Instructional Boundary Management

List of Tables

Table 1: The Proposed Four Key Elements of Instructional Leadership Deriving From Prevalent Frameworks of Instructional Leadership

Table 2: The Four Key Elements of Instructional Leadership as Expressed in Prevalent Frameworks of School Leadership

Foreword

A close colleague of mine once said that the concept of instructional leadership for school leaders is very problematic because it typically has nothing to do with "instruction" and nothing to do with "leadership." I have tended to agree with this concerning and troublesome assessment of the state of our field. This was my view however, until I read this book.

I have known Haim Shaked for years as a gifted educational practitioner, scholar, and leader of a higher education institution. Haim's insights, presented in this new book, indicate that the field has rallied around the importance of instructional leadership for school leaders, and has come to understand that instructional leadership indeed does have a great deal to do with both "instruction" and "leadership."

Haim elevates the notion of instructional leadership with his own research and leadership experiences. In so doing, Haim presents the DNA for instructional leadership, interweaving seamlessly the strands of instruction and leadership. It is this weaving, or the intersection of these two strands, that *are* the imperative for school leadership today. He presents heretofore disconnected views and theories of both instruction and leadership, to create the DNA of instructional leadership.

The two strands of the DNA—instruction and leadership—are developed throughout the book. The beginning of the book in Part I, infuses Lee Shulman's concept of pedagogical content knowledge into the work of school leaders. When was the last time a deeply rooted conception of teaching and learning and instruction was presented at the beginning of a book on school leadership? Haim does not stop there with instruction, but then moves toward the leadership imperative, a compelling discussion of relationships and systems thinking in the work of instructional leadership.

Haim presents concepts and insightful perspectives with vignettes and examples of actions and practices from school principals, such as a focus on standards, curriculum, and assessment. The vignettes bring to life the notion of weaving instruction and leadership together.

My favorite part of the book is the section on the inhibitors to the practice of instructional leadership in Part II. These insights are both original and provocative. Organizational theorists have written about these challenges in organizational leadership, such as goal displacement (a focus on educational outcomes or student belonging, but not both), but now we have direct explanations and applications to schools. School leaders will see themselves in these descriptions but will now also be able to identify and address them with purpose and focus.

New for me, is the notion of the clan culture as an inhibitor. This chapter illuminates that close, comfortable, familiar relationships in schools, often applauded and lauded as a prerequisite for effective leadership and school improvement, have important downsides as well. In the clan culture, for example, it is often difficult for school leaders to focus on improvement efforts, such as classroom observations, lest they upset the delicate balance of relationships motivated exclusively on feeling comfortable. This is a cautionary tale for all school leaders; close relationships cannot come at the expense of leadership for school improvement. Feeling good cannot replace "doing good."

The final part of the book, Part III, acknowledges and embraces the interplay between the practice of instructional leadership and the inhibitors, by understanding the paradoxes inherent in instructional leadership. An explanation of paradoxes helps school leaders work through the inhibitors. "Through a paradoxical approach, leaders provide a guiding direction while emphasizing the need to address, adjust to, and excel at managing tensions." (p. 118).

In an important and influential article on instructional leadership, "How School Leadership Influences Student Learning: A Test of "The Four Paths Model," Ken Leithwood and colleagues (2020) studied the relational, emotional, organizational, and family pathways of leadership, claiming that leadership flows through these pathways to influence student learning.[1] One of the conclusions of this research, not unexpectedly, is the complex nature of the interrelationships among these multiple pathways for school improvement. The authors called for more research. This new book, with its focus on the weaving together of instruction and leadership, presents a powerful response to the call for research. Instructional leadership is indeed the DNA of school leadership.

This book deserves a careful read as it presents a clear and useful set of insights on how to understand and practice instructional leadership in the ever-changing context of education today.

Ellen B. Goldring
Patricia and Rodes Hart Chair
Professor of Education Policy and Leadership
Executive Associate Dean
Peabody College of Education and Human Development,
Vanderbilt University

NOTE

1. Leithwood, K., Sun, J., & Schumacker, R. (2020). How school leadership influences student learning: A test of "The four paths model." Educational Administration Quarterly, 56(4), 570–599.

Preface

The extant corpus of empirical research on instructional leadership, which may be succinctly explained as school leadership that prioritizes teaching and learning development and therefore requires school leaders' extensive and direct involvement in improving instruction and curriculum, is undoubtedly broad. Are there still gaps in the research-informed knowledge base available on instructional leadership that need to be narrowed? Is there anything left to innovate on a subject that has been researched for so many years?

This book claims so. From my perspective, there is much room for new explorations about this topic. Specifically, this book concentrates on the application of instructional leadership. The existing research literature on instructional leadership examines mainly the components, procedures, and mechanisms of instructional leadership and its influence on school performance and students' academic results. In contrast, leaders' applications of instructional leadership have not been sufficiently discussed. This book seeks to narrow this gap by answering the questions of what supports the application of instructional leadership, what may hinder it, and where instructional leadership is still being applied incompletely.

One might think that leaders' application of instructional leadership does not need to occupy a central place in the research literature because it is not problematic and does not involve challenges or difficulties. However, that is not the case. Despite long-standing efforts by researchers, policymakers, and educators to campaign for instructional leadership's prioritization as possibly the most critical component of the school principal's role, several studies have shown that the time devoted by principals to instructional leadership activities remains insufficient (see Chapter 4 below). Considering the substantial efforts that diverse professionals have invested over many decades to encourage and support principals' instructional leadership, these extremely disappointing statistics make the research on instructional leadership application most necessary.

Why do principals find it difficult to put instructional leadership into action? What can help them overcome the challenges involved in applying instructional leadership? What functions of instructional leadership do school leaders tend to sidestep?

Although some researchers have discussed such questions (e.g., Goldring et al., 2008, 2015, 2020; Hallinger & Murphy, 2013; Murphy et al., 2016; Prytula et al., 2013), available knowledge is still limited to the how, why, who, when, and where of applying instructional leadership, calling for further research literature. This is precisely the purpose of this book: to help fill knowledge gaps by providing additional research-informed literature on instructional leadership's applications.

The central assertion of this book is that instructional leadership can be put into practice effectively only if the complexity of the school is taken into account. A school is inherently a complex organization, which involves a vast assortment of interacting purposes, people, and activities. As such, it often encounters significant dilemmas and conflicts, which are rooted in the school's variety of needs, norms, and priorities. These are further intensified due to the presence of a diversity of stakeholders who maintain different, or even contradicting, desires, views, expectations, and demands, and who are affected by a wide range of contextual influences.

The clear expectation of researchers, policymakers, and educators from school leaders to become instructional leaders has been a valuable first step toward making instructional leadership an everyday reality in schools. However, a narrow focus on the application of instructional leadership while ignoring how the school's complexity shapes the work of the school leader is inadequate as it does not allow us to see the big picture. Instructional leadership is implemented by school leaders who run schools consisting of intersecting elements. Therefore, its application is possible only if we recognize the many networks operating in the intra- and extra-school worlds and their mutual effects.

This book seeks to understand some of the highly nonlinear relationships in the school that have direct and indirect connections to instructional leadership's application. To this end, the book inquires into topics such as the complicated system of interactions at play between instructional leadership application and principal-teacher relationships; principals' perceptions regarding the fundamental goal of schooling as impacting how they implement instructional leadership; and contextual influences on instructional leadership application, which are associated with the characteristics of parents, community, or national values. Overall, this book suggests a more nuanced understanding of the application of instructional leadership within the complex system that is the school.

It should be noted that early research on instructional leadership saw it as the role of the principal alone and therefore explored only the principal's practices that support effective teaching and learning. In those early days, an overly "heroic" perception of the role of the principal prevented researchers from fully recognizing the decentralized nature of leadership in schools. Over the years, however, it became clear that instructional leadership should be applied by others in addition to the principal: school middle leaders and all teachers.

This book is mainly dedicated to the principal's perspective on instructional leadership application, not because of a belief that instructional leadership is irrelevant to middle leaders and other teachers but because the head school principal plays an essential role and confronts unique challenges in applying this leadership approach. Although instructional leadership should be distributed through networks of influence at different school levels, principals' particular significance makes them worthy of comprehensive attention and guidance in navigating the specific complexities they face every day in applying instructional leadership.

Basing this book on a series of studies conducted over the past five years among principals working in the Israeli school system, I am fully aware that instructional leadership application is inseparable from the context in which the school is situated. No two schools are exactly the same, nor are national education systems. Although schools and national education systems may have the same goals and policies, their ability to fulfill their aspirations is intensely affected by their unique conditions.

Several chapters of this book examine contextual influences on instructional leadership (see Chapters 5–7), seeking to explore not only "what works" but also "what works in a particular context." However, the findings of the studies conducted in Israel are presented in this book in a way that can be used by school leaders in different countries, and literature from a variety of continents is utilized. An effort has been made to generalize the primary claims of the book so that they can fit a wide range of education systems around the world.

Specifically, I have mainly conducted interview research because face-to-face, semi-structured conversations are widely held to be a valuable tool for uncovering study participants' beliefs, experiences, and worldviews. Therefore, I have had the profound privilege of becoming closely acquainted with the professional lives and educational work of hundreds of school leaders who have generously shared their insights and experiences during interviews and focus groups.

Enabling school leaders to use their own words when describing the application of instructional leadership, this book is richly peppered with examples taken from the realities of school life and brings ample quotes from active principals' own voices. However, for ethical reasons, study participants were assured of confidentiality. Thus, all the principals' names in this book are pseudonyms, and identifying details were changed as needed.

My studies' findings were first published as journal articles and then formed the basis for this book. Turning the articles into book chapters allowed me to expand on explanations of the findings. Moreover, bringing this work together under one cover makes it possible to step back and see the whole picture, the "forest," instead of focusing only on its parts, the "trees."

This book opens with an introductory chapter that defines instructional leadership, describes its development over the years, differentiates it from other leadership approaches, and marks its benefits. Then, it identifies four key elements of instructional leadership and the influence of this model on our understanding of school leadership in general. Then, the book consists of four parts.

Part I deals with the enablers of instructional leadership application. First, Chapter 1 delves into the components of the knowledge required for instructional leadership application. Then, Chapter 2 explores the intrapersonal and interpersonal relationships needed to apply instructional leadership. Next, Chapter 3 presents systems thinking, which puts the study of wholes before that of parts, and proposes how this type of thinking can act as an essential facilitator of several vital functions for instructional leaders.

Part II examines the inhibitory factors at play in instructional leadership, which may offer some explanations as to why not all principals fully apply this leadership approach despite vast encouragement to do so. Chapter 4 first reviews the barriers discussed in the existing literature and then explores a new type of barrier—principals' inhibitory perceptions. Based on this, Chapter 5 gives special attention to the clan culture that can typify some schools, which can act as a barrier to applying some of the functions of instructional leadership. Next, Chapter 6 raises the question of how the national context for educational systems may inhibit the application of instructional leadership. As a case in point, this chapter discusses low power distance, which refers to the degree to which a specific society expects and accepts that power is unevenly distributed among people. Touching upon another contextual issue, Chapter 7 examines the application of instructional leadership in rural areas inasmuch as education in such regions is often relatively inferior compared to urban regions in many countries around the globe.

Part III delves into some of the main situations in schools where instructional leadership is often applied incompletely. Chapter 8 elucidates why principals tend to turn teacher evaluation into a useless component of instructional leadership. Chapter 9 explains why the vital task of ensuring that the "right" teachers are on staff is rarely mentioned in the literature as an inherent component of instructional leadership. Chapter 10 concentrates on assistant principals, who are often considered in the research literature to be "forgotten leaders." To expand available knowledge on their application efforts, this chapter investigates the boundaries of instructional leadership in assistant principals.

Part IV of the book offers some tools for instructional leaders in the form of the paradoxical approach. As presented in Chapter 11, one way to deal with the factors that may inhibit the application of instructional leadership is through the paradoxical approach, which advocates a "both/and" way of dealing with conflicting demands. To further illustrate the paradoxical approach, Chapter 12 then inquires into the overlap between instructional leadership and boundary management, which seeks to regulate the boundary separating the school from its environment. This chapter proposes a new area of school leadership—instructional boundary management—which is a synthesis of these two different complementary frameworks.

This book ends with an epilogue, which summarizes what this book adds to the existing literature. Instructional leadership does not operate in a vacuum but rather within the complex system that is the school. Thus, the epilogue explores some of the ways in which the complicated nature of schools frequently influences the application of instructional leadership. Identifying the intricacies involved in the implementation of instructional leadership and finding ways to deal with such complexity may be seen as a unique contribution of this book.

Overall, this book presents recent findings that offer new knowledge about instructional leadership application. Researchers of educational leadership, management, and administration worldwide will find that the book opens novel avenues for research on the application of instructional leadership. In addition, the text will be of interest to faculty members who teach various courses as part of academic programs in educational leadership and policy, principal preparation programs, and professional development. The book may also evoke interest across a wide gamut of policymakers and educational leaders who want to better understand their role in enhancing today's education systems.

Practically, it offers significant suggestions for how to apply instructional leadership and which actions can be taken in order to realize the promise of school improvement—with concrete recommendations proposed at the end of each chapter, not only geared to principals themselves but also to their supervisors and educators. I hope this book will be widely used by all those connected to and involved in the critical endeavor of educational leadership.

REFERENCES

Goldring, E., Grissom, J. A., Neumerski, C. M., Blissett, R., Murphy, J., & Porter, A. (2020). Increasing principals' time on instructional leadership: Exploring the SAM® process. *Journal of Educational Administration, 58*(1), 19–37.

Goldring, E., Grissom, J. A., Neumerski, C. M., Murphy, J., Blissett, R., & Porter, A. (2015). *Making time for instructional leadership*. Wallace Foundation. http://www.wallacefoundation.org/knowledge-center/Pages/Making-Time-for-Instructional-Leadership.aspx

Goldring, E., Huff, J., May, H., & Camburn, E. (2008). School context and individual characteristics: What influences principal practice? *Journal of Educational Administration, 46*(3), 332–352.

Hallinger, P., & Murphy, J. F. (2013). Running on empty? Finding the time and capacity to lead learning. *Bulletin of the National Association of Secondary School Principals, 97*(1), 5–21.

Murphy, J., Neumerski, C. M., Goldring, E., Grissom, J., & Porter, A. (2016). Bottling fog? The quest for instructional management. *Cambridge Journal of Education, 46*(4), 455–471.

Prytula, M., Noonan, B., & Hellsten, L. (2013). Toward instructional leadership: Principals perceptions of large-scale assessment in schools. *Canadian Journal of Educational Administration and Policy, 140*, 1–30.

Acknowledgments

I would like to express my sincere gratitude to my esteemed colleagues, who partnered with me in writing some of the articles on which this book is based and who generously permitted me to share the results of our joint studies in this book. My appreciation goes out to Prof. Philip Hallinger, who is clearly one of the most prolific and influential scholars in the field of instructional leadership; Prof. Chen Schechter, under whose supervision I wrote my doctoral dissertation and with whom I have since collaborated on various research activities; Prof. Zehavit Gross, for whom I am grateful that in addition to her many research pursuits she also serves as chair of the Academic Council at my college; Prof. Jeffrey Glanz, my ex-employer whose endless passion for research and writing is a source of inspiration for me; and Dr. Pascale Benoliel, whose thorough academic work ensures the continuation of her contribution to research on educational leadership and policy.

My most tremendous thanks are to my family, for all the support you have shown me. You are always there for me. Much of what I have learned over the years came from being a husband to my beloved wife Tali, a father to our wonderful children, and a grandfather to our delightful grandchildren. Without your encouragement and sympathetic ears, I would not have had a chance of coming this far. Words cannot express how much I love you.

Series Editor's Introduction

Why a new book series on school leadership, and what does this particular series have to offer among the many fine books already published in the field of school and educational leadership?

Research over the past decade has confirmed what many educators, policy makers, think tanks, and others viscerally knew—that leadership makes a difference for a host of dependent variables, including the most important one, student achievement. Additional research is needed, however, to more fully refine and uncover how, in fact, school leaders make a difference in a host of other areas. The answers to additional research questions will offer further legitimacy and draw greater attention to the field of educational leadership. The questions (which can possibly prompt potential authors to submit a book proposal) include the following, among others:

- What effect does the continuing increased accountability and high-stakes testing have on teacher morale, principal self-efficacy, and student achievement?
- What additional information do we need about systems thinking and its relationship to school leadership?
- What are the specific gender differences as related to leading schools?
- What is the precise role played by school leaders in fostering inclusive educational practices?
- How is social justice best fostered by school leaders?
- What specific educational leadership strategies reduce the Black/White achievement gap?
- How might school leaders implement an effective data-driven decision-making process in their schools?
- What are the critical factors affecting high performance among principals?
- What is the role of school leaders in reducing school violence?
- How do leadership practices positively influence school-community partnerships?

- What is the association between transformational leadership and teacher self-efficacy?
- How does shared leadership affect school morale and productivity?
- How do various types or forms of leadership impact organizational effectiveness?
- What are the social, cultural, political, and historical factors that influence the practice of educational leadership in different countries?
- How do leadership practices differ in differing contexts, social, cultural, or otherwise?
- What are the theoretical and practical differences among educational administration, management, and leadership?
- Why is an international perspective so critical for better understanding the challenges of leading schools in the 21st century?
- How can school leaders address race and identity, bias and privilege, and racialized current events?
- How can comparative research studies help us better understand educational leadership?
- What can we learn from studying educational leaders beyond the school level (e.g., district and Ministry (or Board) of Education leaders)?
- To what extent does emotional labor impact educational leaders?
- How can principals encourage action research and other alternatives to supervision to enhance teacher professional growth?
- How do school leaders effectively implement new technologies not just for the sake of technology but to deepen learning and provide better support for teachers?
- What are the consequences of workload on school leaders (e.g., the principal, or others) on effectiveness as a leader?
- What are the challenges that school leaders face in differing regional contexts?
- How do school leaders develop the skills and knowledge they need to understand teachers' and students' needs and effectively guide learning?
- How do effective school leaders balance administrative duties with instructional priorities?
- What new educational management strategies can help teachers better confront classroom behavioral issues?
- How do school leaders coordinate curriculum and instructional initiatives across schools?
- Given time and budget constraints, how can school leaders find the resources to support an artful education (music, dance, creative writing, etc.) for all students?
- How do increased efforts to promote teacher leadership impact the work of principals and their assistants?

- What new innovative ideas can principals implement to deal with the increasingly complex landscape of curriculum today?
- How can principals support teacher-led professional development?
- What is the role of identity in fostering principal self-efficacy?
- How can school leaders help schools become more integral to their surrounding communities—and how can they better leverage community resources and connections to support their students and teachers?
- How can we better balance interest and work in instructional leadership with other important leadership responsibilities?
- How can districts support assistant principals and prepare new principals as they take the helm of the school?
- How do we induct and sustain good principals?
- How can we best prepare future school leaders?

Most fundamentally, the Bridging Theory and Practice: The Rowman & Littlefield School Leadership Series is premised on the need to connect theory to practice. Each of these questions rely on a sound theoretical base that has important, if not critical, relevance to the world of practice. This international series, in other words, reflects the latest cutting-edge theories and practices in school leadership that attempt to bridge the perennial divide between theory and practice.

Although we look to publish manuscripts that have relevance to an international audience, we will accept more localized research that might only be applicable in a specific context. The manuscript, of course, must meet the rigors of academic research and have significant impact on practice. Feel free to query the Series Editor to react to any ideas.

The series motto is framed after Kurt Lewin's famous statement, and we paraphrase, that there is no sound theory without practice, and no good practice that is not framed on some theory. Authors are expected to illustrate the intimate and integral connection between the two divides. In this respect, we are unique because we do not accept proposals that are "heavy" on one side or the other; rather we look for manuscripts that are intellectually engaging, with a sound theoretical base, yet firmly grounded in the daily lives of school leaders. I welcome readers to join the effort to increase knowledge in our field and affect daily school practice by submitting a proposal on any of the topics mentioned above, or any other relevant ones. Feel free to communicate with the series editor via email at yosglanz@gmail.com

As Series Editor, I would like to take this opportunity to thank my latest Advisory Board, listed below, for their efforts in seeing the series to fruition. Their feedback to the authors and the editor were instrumental in crafting a well-researched, practical, and readable volume.

Köksal Banoğlu, Chief Project Executive at Maltepe District Governorship—Istanbul—Turkey
Clair T. Berube, Virginia Wesleyan University—Virginia Beach, VA —USA
Yin Cheong Cheng, The Education University of Hong Kong—Tai Po —Hong Kong
Mary Lynne Derrington, University of Tennessee—Knoxville, TN —USA
Sedat Gumus, Necmettin Erbakan University—Konya —Turkey
Sonya D. Hayes, University of Tennessee—Knoxville, TN —USA
Helen M. Hazi, West Virginia University at Morgantown—West Virginia —USA
Albert Jimenez, Kennesaw State University—Kennesaw, GA —USA
Benjamin Kutsyuruba, Queen's University—Kingston, ON —Canada
Orly Shapira-Lishchinsky, Bar Ilan University—Ramat Gan —Israel
Jane Wilkinson, Monash University—Victoria —Australia

Special acknowledgement is extended to Tom Koerner (Vice President and Publisher for Education Issues) and Kira Hall (Assistant Editor) for their support. I hope this volume and the series will receive wide acknowledgement for making a difference in the field of educational leadership.

As Series Editor, I am excited to introduce this latest volume of our series authored by Professor Haim Shaked, among the most renowned and foremost scholars in the field of educational leadership. He is a prolific researcher who has examined leadership issues, particularly of an instructional nature, in a variety of contexts. This work fits beautifully with the theme of this series that combines theory with practice. He masterfully weaves extant research and theory in the field with practical ways practitioners can implement his ideas. As a former school principal himself, he understands the world of practice and realizes the instructional challenges leaders face.

I am without doubt that Prof. Shaked's work here will find a receptive audience because instructional leadership has dominated the research literature over the past decade. School boards and Ministries (Boards) of Education, today, have demanding expectations that principals and other school leaders attend to and address critical issues of teaching and learning, rather than delegate them to others, or worse, eschew them. *New Explorations for Instructional Leaders: How Principals Can Promote Teaching and Learning Effectively* amalgamates previous work in the field with the latest and newest ideas that provide school leaders with practical ways to improve teaching and learning, and thereby, increase student achievement.

I believe this book with become the primer and required reading for all prospective and current school leaders. I would even go so far as to say that it will become a classic in the field of school leadership.

Jeffrey Glanz
May 6, 2022

Introduction

What Is Instructional Leadership?

ABSTRACT

To lay the groundwork for this book on instructional leadership's application, this introduction is devoted to its fundamentals. To begin, the introduction provides answers to some rudimentary questions about this leadership approach's definition, development, and premises. Then, the conceptual frameworks outlining instructional leadership are discussed to furnish readers with the essentials of the "language" of instructional leadership. Specifically, four key elements of instructional leadership are proposed: instructional vision, instructional program, instructional climate, and teacher development.

ANSWERING THE BASIC QUESTIONS OF INSTRUCTIONAL LEADERSHIP

What is a broad definition of "instructional leadership?" Instructional leadership can be construed as an educational leadership approach whereby school leaders are continually and actively involved in a wide range of activities aiming to improve teaching and learning for all students. Simply put, instructional leadership requires school principals to focus their efforts directly onto the core activities of schooling—teaching and learning—so that students can achieve academic success.

According to this approach, principals are expected to demonstrate ongoing deep involvement in promoting best instructional practices and intense engagement in curricular and instructional issues. Thus, top priority should be given by leaders to student learning and academic results, while everything else—including traditional administrative and other tasks—should be considered of lesser priority.

How has school leadership changed over time? In the past, principals were primarily responsible for managerial and administrative tasks, such as ensuring student safety, enforcing school policies, and maintaining facilities' maintenance. Managerial tasks such as ordering supplies and creating bus schedules were common daily tasks of the principal. In contrast, contemporary principals are no longer seen as mere managerial or organizational administrators; at present, instructional leadership is one of their most important responsibilities. Even though today's principals do remain involved in many tasks that tend to distract from this vital effort, effective principals focus directly on instruction because they know that such a focus will impact students the most.

What historical developments for instructional leadership can be traced? Among the multiple theories and models that have emerged across the research literature on school leadership to help describe and understand how principals influence school performance, instructional leadership is the most frequently studied conceptual framework over past decades. Several landmark stages may be identified along the long-term processes that shaped instructional leadership into its current prominence as an educational leadership approach.

Perhaps the first landmark was the series of articles published in *Bulletin of the National Association of Secondary School Principals* in the mid-20th century in the United States, urging principals to demonstrate instructional leadership (e.g., Corey et al., 1951; Spears, 1941; Willey, 1942). The second landmark was likely the keen interest channeled toward achieving "effective schools" in the 1980s, which lent significant support to the claim that the principal's role as an instructional leader rather than mere administrator was essential to school efficiency.

The third landmark stage driving principals to direct their work more explicitly toward improving teaching and learning was the "accountability" movement in educational policymaking that emerged at the end of the 20th century, which gave rise to an increasing emphasis on the measurable academic outcomes of students and schools. The most recent stage can be identified as occurring at the beginning of the 21st century, when instructional leadership became widespread not only in the United States but also in many other countries around the globe, in part because of internationally shared achievement tests.

How do instructional leaders promote their goals? Although principals as instructional leaders are central figures in promoting high academic achievement levels for students, their influence on students is mainly indirect, mediated by factors such as the instructional program and the school culture, and most of all by teachers' teaching strategies. Principals who enact instructional leadership make sure that teachers take full advantage of instructional time for effective, high-quality teaching and that teachers develop professionally on an ongoing basis.

Therefore, the instructional leadership framework is based on the close connections identified between teachers' quality of instruction and students' academic results. We know for sure that teaching quality is the most important school-related factor influencing student outcomes (e.g., Darling-Hammond, 2000; Goe & Stickler, 2008; Stronge et al., 2007). Namely, schoolchildren's achievements depend crucially on their teachers' effectiveness, more than many other school factors like curricular programs or student grouping patterns. Consistently high-quality instruction, which is a prerequisite for student results, requires constant nurturing and guidance by the principal as an instructional leader.

Who can and should be an instructional leader? Instructional leadership does not concern only the principal or just the members of the senior management team. Whether their roles are assigned formally or shared informally, all school middle leaders also need to fulfill instructional leadership roles, ranging from organizational functions like department heads to instructional functions like literacy coaches or book study-group facilitators.

In fact, all teachers need to become instructional leaders, reaching out and sharing effective practices with others in order to benefit all students. Therefore, instructional leadership should be seen as an organizational characteristic of the entire school. However, for the most part, this book concentrates on principals' instructional leadership to illustrate their specific role in applying this leadership approach in schools.

How does instructional leadership fit in with transformational leadership? The "instructional" leadership approach has differentiated itself from the "transformational" leadership approach. Under transformational leadership, principals do not practice the everyday guidance of curriculum and instruction or the monitoring of student learning. They concentrate on building trust, supporting the needs of teachers, and transferring the school's goals to the staff's personal goals.

Under instructional leadership, on the other hand, principals work to build a positive climate through professional development and coordination and through the attainment of instructional goals. Interestingly, Robinson and her colleagues' (2008) meta-analysis of research on effective school leadership showed that the average effect of instructional leadership on student outcomes was three to four times higher than that of transformational leadership.

Interestingly, Marks and Printy (2003, see also Bowers, 2020) argued that while there are schools with high transformational leadership and low instructional leadership, there are no schools with high instructional leadership and low transformational leadership. Thus, transformational leadership may be considered necessary but insufficient for instructional leadership.

What ethical and social considerations are linked to this leadership framework? An instructional leadership mindset includes a profound moral purpose focused on promoting learning experiences and opportunities for all students. Social injustice often characterizes today's Western schools, where white, heterosexual, middle-class, and physically able students reach higher achievements, drop out less, and are more likely to attend higher-education institutions than their counterparts from other races, gender orientations, socioeconomic backgrounds, and disability statuses.

Instructional leadership contributes to social justice because instructional leaders are those who seek to narrow inequality gaps in academic outcomes, creating a learning climate that provides all students with equal opportunities regardless of various possibly marginalizing characteristics. As social justice leaders, instructional leaders cultivate effective, egalitarian, and socially responsible learning and accountability practices for all students. Instructional leaders are, therefore, also social justice leaders—referring to leaders who ensure that social justice concepts are realized in schools so as to provide fair and equal opportunities (see Shaked, 2020).

Have the effects of instructional leadership been empirically demonstrated? Research has affirmed the efficacy of instructional leadership with respect to achieving the goals of student achievement and school improvement (e.g., Mitchell et al., 2015; O'Donnell & White, 2005; Shatzer et al., 2014). Thus, researchers have clearly shown instructional leadership to be a crucial factor in facilitating and promoting students' academic progress.

In addition, research studies have pinpointed instructional leadership as a pivotal function of principals who achieve promising school improvement outcomes. A wide body of research literature from the 1980s through the present has clearly associated instructional leadership with positive school outcomes, including higher teaching quality and improved student achievements.

This link has been demonstrated in various organizational contexts such as in elementary, junior high, and high schools as well as across public, private, and public charter schools. This connection has also been demonstrated in diverse geo-social contexts such as urban and suburban schools. (See also Chapter 7 about instructional leadership in rural areas, which has not yet been sufficiently researched.)

What is expected of instructional leaders today? These empirical links identified between principals' active involvement in instruction, its high quality, and the achievements of students have led to scholars' broadly voiced call for contemporary principals to see instructional leadership as their top priority. Thus, scholars and practitioners alike contend that contemporary school principals should enact instructional leadership as one of their central, core responsibilities. Today's principals are expected to, and even required to, assume a prominent role as instructional leaders who emphasize the teaching and learning aspects of school leadership and have a hand in a wide array of curricular and instructional issues.

CONCEPTUAL FRAMEWORKS OF INSTRUCTIONAL LEADERSHIP

Over the years, researchers have attempted to capture the meaning of instructional leadership via several frameworks. The framework presented by Hallinger and Murphy (1985) is the most common one utilized in the instructional leadership research literature (Hallinger & Wang, 2015). It consists of three dimensions that include ten functions.

In the first dimension, *defining the school mission,* the instructional leader is expected to hold responsibility for ensuring a clear mission for the school, which can be obtained by focusing on the academic progress of all students and by sharing this mission with the school community. That is, this dimension asks the principal to perform two main functions: (1) Framing the school's instructional goals; and (2) Communicating those goals to all necessary parties.

The second dimension, *managing the instructional program,* refers to the principals' ultimate responsibility for regulating and controlling the school's academic curricula. This dimension comprises three primary functions: (3) Coordinating the school's curriculum; (4) Supervising and evaluating instruction; and (5) Monitoring students' progress.

The third dimension, *developing a positive school learning climate,* refers to the instructional leader's responsibility for creating a culture of ongoing improvement as well as high standards and expectations for both students and teachers. This dimension is broken down into five functions for the school principal: (6) Protecting instructional time from threats; (7) Providing incentives to motivate teachers; (8) Providing incentives to encourage students' learning; (9) Promoting staff members' continual professional development; and (10) Maintaining high visibility for quality interactions with teachers and students.

Quite similar to Hallinger and Murphy (1985), the framework outlined by Weber (1996) delineates five dimensions of instructional leadership: (1) Defining the school's mission; (2) Managing curriculum and instruction; (3) Supervising teaching; (4) Monitoring student progress; and (5) Assessing the instructional climate.

Blase and Blase (2000) explored the perspectives of teachers on principals' instructional leadership, focusing on the link between instructional leadership and teachers. Based on an open-ended questionnaire, they identified two themes and 11 strategies of instructional leadership that influences change in teacher practice. The first theme was talking with teachers to promote reflection. This theme included five strategies: (1) Making suggestions; (2) Giving feedback; (3) Modeling; (4) Using inquiry and soliciting advice and opinions; and (5) Giving praise.

The second theme was promoting professional growth. This theme incorporated six strategies: (1) Emphasizing the study of teaching and learning; (2) Supporting collaboration efforts among educators; (3) Developing coaching relationships among educators; (4) Encouraging and supporting redesign of programs; (5) Applying the principles of adult learning, growth, and development to all phases of staff development; and (6) Implementing action research to inform instructional decision making.

Based on a systematic, broad literature review, Stronge and his colleagues (2008) were able to summarize five essential features of instructional leadership that principals have been found to apply to meet instructional ends. These five include: (1) Building and sustaining a school vision—developing a school vision that sets clear learning goals and gaining community support for those goals; (2) Sharing leadership—distributing leadership roles by strengthening the expertise of teacher leaders to enhance school performance; (3) Leading a learning community—steering a collaborative community of professional learners that provides meaningful staff development; (4) Using data to make instructional decisions—collecting and using facts and evidence in instructional decision making; and (5) Monitoring curriculum and instruction—keeping tabs on and promoting the implementation of curricula and quality teaching methods by spending time in classes.

Taking these major instructional leadership frameworks together, I propose that the salient points at the core of instructional leadership can be synthesized. Let's identify these as the following four key elements of instructional leadership: (1) *Instructional vision*—building and mobilizing support for a school vision based on goals for student learning and results; (2) *Instructional program*—coordinating, supervising, guiding, and monitoring teaching and learning in the school; (3) *Instructional climate*—creating a positive, achievement-oriented academic environment; and (4) *Developing teachers*—ensuring that faculty members continue to strengthen their practice throughout their career. Table 1 illustrates how the dimensions, functions, and features of instructional leadership, which make up the existing frameworks, fall under the proposed four key elements of instructional leadership.

Existing common frameworks of school leadership in general do not always explicitly refer to or revolve around the instructional leadership

Table 1: The Proposed Four Key Elements of Instructional Leadership Deriving From Prevalent Frameworks of Instructional Leadership

Key element	Frameworks' dimensions/functions/themes/strategies			
	Hallinger & Murphy, 1985	Weber, 1996	Blase & Blase (2000)	Stronge et al., 2008
Instructional vision	Defining the school mission Framing school goals Communicating school goals	Defining the school mission		Building and sustaining a school vision
Instructional program	Managing the instructional program Coordinating the curriculum Supervising and evaluating instruction	Managing curriculum and instruction Supervising teaching	Talking with teachers to promote reflection Making suggestions Giving feedback Modeling Using inquiry and soliciting advice and opinions	Monitoring curriculum and instruction Using data to make instructional decisions
	Monitoring student progress	Monitoring student progress		

Key element	Hallinger & Murphy, 1985	Weber, 1996	Blase & Blase (2000)	Stronge et al., 2008
Instructional climate	Developing a positive school learning climate Protecting instructional time Providing incentives for teachers Providing incentives for learning Maintaining high visibility Promoting professional development	Assessing the instructional climate	Giving praise	
Developing teachers			Promoting professional growth Emphasizing the study of teaching and learning Supporting collaboration efforts Developing coaching relationships Encouraging redesign of programs applying the principles of adult learning, growth, and development Implementing action research	Leading a learning community Sharing leadership

approach. However, examination of how scholars do conceptualize and investigate school leaders' work indicates that the proposed four key instructional leadership elements deriving from the existing literature—instructional vision, instructional program, instructional climate, and developing teachers—also appear to underlie these other frameworks.

For example, as presented in Table 2, four of the five school leadership dimensions that Robinson (2007) described as affecting a range of student outcomes can be seen as coinciding with the four key instructional leadership elements: (1) Establishing goals and expectations; (2) Planning, coordinating, and evaluating the teaching and curriculum; (3) Ensuring an orderly and supportive environment; and (4) Promoting and participating in teacher learning and development. The last of Robinson's dimensions, (5) Resourcing strategically, may be seen as serving the previous dimensions by aligning resource selection and allocation with prioritized goals of teaching and professional development.

Likewise, Murphy and his colleagues (2007) proposed a research-based model and taxonomy of behaviors targeting "leadership for learning." Six of the eight proposed school leadership behaviors appear to align with the proposed four key instructional leadership elements: (1) Vision for learning—developing vision, articulating vision, implementing vision, and stewarding vision; (2) Instructional program—acquiring knowledge and increasing involvement, hiring and allocating staff, supporting staff, and protecting instructional time; (3) Curricular program—acquiring knowledge and increasing involvement, setting expectations and standards, providing opportunities to learn, and aligning curriculum; (4) Assessment program—acquiring knowledge and increasing involvement, establishing assessment procedures, monitoring instruction and curriculum, and using data; (5) Communities of learning—promoting professional development, establishing communities of professional practice, and creating community anchored schools; and (6) Organizational culture—emphasizing production, cultivating learning environment, enabling personalized environment, and supporting continuous improvement. One more leadership behavior, (7) Resource acquisition and use (i.e., acquiring resources, allocating resources, and using resources) may be considered as supporting the previous behaviors. The last of Murphy and colleagues' suggested leadership-for-learning behaviors, (8) Social advocacy (i.e., engaging stakeholders, ensuring diversity, recognizing environmental context, and adhering to ethics) is about how to make use of instructional leadership behaviors for the sake of achieving social justice and equity in education.

Leithwood and Louis (2011) pointed to four core school leadership practices, three of which seem to coincide with the proposed four key instructional leadership elements (see Table 2): (1) Setting directions—defining

Table 2: The Four Key Elements of Instructional Leadership as Expressed in Prevalent Frameworks of School Leadership

Key element	Frameworks' functions/features			
	Robinson, 2007	Murphy et al., 2007	Leithwood & Louis, 2011	Halverson & Kelley, 2017
Instructional vision	Establishing goals and expectations	Vision for learning	Setting directions	Focus on learning
Instructional program	Planning, coordinating, and evaluating teaching and the curriculum	Instructional program Curricular program Assessment program	Managing the instructional program	Monitoring teaching and learning
Instructional climate	Ensuring an orderly and supportive environment	Organizational culture		Maintaining a safe and effective environment
Developing teachers	Promoting and participating in teacher learning and development	Communities of learning	Developing people	Building nested learning communities
Other	Resourcing strategically	Resource acquisition and use Social advocacy	Redesigning the organization	Acquiring and allocating resources

organizational purposes; (2) Developing people—expanding the capacities of organizational members to pursue these directions; and (3) Managing the instructional program—improving teaching and curriculum. Leithwood and Louis's recommended fourth practice, (4) Redesigning the organization (i.e., modifying the organization to align with and support members' work), seeks to ensure that instructional leadership will not be satisfied with small and specific advances but rather will strive for a total change of the school as an organization.

A few years later, Halverson and Kelley (2017) presented a five-domain model of school leadership. Four of these domains appear to correspond with the proposed four key instructional leadership elements (see Table 2): (1) Focus on learning; (2) Monitoring teaching and learning; (3) Building nested learning communities; and (4) Maintaining a safe and effective environment. Similar to the frameworks mentioned above, the last domain, (5) Acquiring and allocating resources, may be viewed as at the service of the other domains.

Overall, the various leadership frameworks presented here clearly indicate the central place occupied by the proposed four key elements of instructional leadership—instructional vision, instructional program, instructional climate, and developing teachers. Therefore, the proposed four key elements of instructional leadership should be seen as fundamental components of school leadership conceptualizations.

CONCLUSION

This introduction provides answers to some basic questions about the definition, development, and assumptions of instructional leadership. Moreover, it proposes four key elements of instructional leadership arising from common frameworks of instructional leadership and effective school leadership. This means that to be effective, school leadership frameworks should be meaningfully based on the key elements of instructional leadership—instructional vision, instructional program, instructional climate, and developing teachers.

REFERENCES

Blase, J., & Blase, J. (2000). Effective instructional leadership: Teachers' perspectives on how principals promote teaching and learning in schools. *Journal of Educational Administration, 38*(2), 130–141.

Bowers, A. J. (2020). *Examining a congruency-typology model of leadership for learning using two-level latent class analysis with TALIS 2018.* OECD Publishing.

Corey, S. M., Wellesley Foshay, A., & Mackenzie, G. N. (1951). Instructional leadership and the perceptions of the individuals involved. *Bulletin of the National Association of Secondary School Principals, 35*(181), 83–91.

Darling-Hammond, L. (2000). Teacher quality and student achievement. *Education Policy Analysis Archives, 8*(1), 1–44.

Goe, L., & Stickler, L. M. (2008). *Teacher quality and student achievement: Making the most of recent research.* National Comprehensive Center for Teacher Quality.

Hallinger, P., & Murphy, J. (1985). Assessing the instructional management behavior of principals. *The Elementary School Journal, 86*(2), 217–247.

Hallinger, P., & Wang, W. C. (2015). *Assessing instructional leadership with the Principal Instructional Management Rating Scale.* Springer.

Halverson, R., & Kelley, C. (2017). *Mapping leadership: The tasks that matter for improving teaching and learning in schools.* Jossey-Bass.

Leithwood, K., & Louis, K. S. (2011). *Linking leadership to student learning.* Jossey-Bass.

Marks, H. M., & Printy, S. M. (2003). Principal leadership and school performance: An integration of transformational and instructional leadership. *Educational Administration Quarterly, 39*(3), 370–397.

Mitchell, R. M., Kensler, L. A., & Tschannen-Moran, M. (2015). Examining the effects of instructional leadership on school academic press and student achievement. *Journal of School Leadership, 25*(2), 223–251.

Murphy, J., Elliott, S. N., Goldring, E., & Porter, A. C. (2007). Leadership for learning: A research-based model and taxonomy of behaviors. *School Leadership and Management, 27*(2), 179–201.

O'Donnell, R. J., & White, G. P. (2005). Within the accountability era: Principals' instructional leadership behaviors and student achievement. *Bulletin of the National Association of Secondary School Principals, 89*(645), 56–71.

Robinson, V. (2007). *School leadership and student outcomes: Identifying what works and why.* Australian Council for Educational Leaders.

Robinson, V. M. J., Lloyd, C. A., & Rowe, K. J. (2008). The impact of leadership on student outcomes: An analysis of the differential effects of leadership types. *Educational Administration Quarterly, 44*(5), 635–674.

Shaked, H. (2020). Social justice leadership, instructional leadership, and the goals of schooling. *International Journal of Educational Management, 34*(1), 81–95.

Shatzer, R. H., Caldarella, P., Hallam, P. R., & Brown, B. L. (2014). Comparing the effects of instructional and transformational leadership on student achievement: Implications for practice. *Educational Management Administration & Leadership, 42*(4), 445–459.

Spears, H. (1941). Can the line-and-staff principle unify instructional leadership? *Bulletin of the National Association of Secondary School Principals, 25*(98), 25–31.

Stronge, J. H., Richard, H. B., & Catano, N. (2008). *Qualities of effective principals.* Association for Supervision and Curriculum Development.

Stronge, J. H., Ward, T. J., Tucker, P. D., & Hindman, J. L. (2007). What is the relationship between teacher quality and student achievement? An exploratory study. *Journal of Personnel Evaluation in Education, 20*(3), 165–184.

Weber, J. (1996). Leading the instructional program. In S. C. Smith & P. K. Piele (Eds.). *School leadership: Handbook for excellence* (2nd ed., pp. 191–224). ERIC Clearinghouse on Educational Management.

Willey, G. S. (1942). Instructional leadership in the junior and senior high schools of Denver. *Bulletin of the National Association of Secondary School Principals, 26*(107), 61–65.

PART I

Enablers of Instructional Leadership Application

The current part of the book explores several important facilitators or enablers of instructional leadership applications. Thus, Chapter 1 identifies the professional knowledge base that principals need to apply this type of leadership approach. Then, Chapter 2 examines the intrapersonal and interpersonal relationships necessary for applying instructional leadership. Chapter 3 introduces systems thinking, which does not try to break systems down into parts in order to understand them but rather concentrates its attention on how the parts act together in networks of interaction. This chapter suggests that systems thinking can serve as an essential facilitator of the key elements characterizing instructional leaders.

Chapter 1

Knowledge Enabling Instructional Leadership Application

ABSTRACT

This chapter utilizes Shulman's (1987) typology of teachers' knowledge base to discuss what types of knowledge enable principals to apply instructional leadership. Research is presented suggesting that instructional leaders ascribe much importance to their General Pedagogical Knowledge and to Knowledge of Learners and Their Characteristics. In addition, they see themselves as making a unique instructional leadership contribution due to their Knowledge of Educational Contexts and Knowledge of Educational Ends. At the same time, they consider the subject-specific areas of knowledge, including Content Knowledge, Pedagogical Content Knowledge, and Curriculum Knowledge, as less necessary for their instructional leadership role. The chapter concludes with practical recommendations regarding the knowledge enabling instructional leadership application.

THE TYPOLOGY OF SHULMAN IN THE CONTEXT OF INSTRUCTIONAL LEADERSHIP APPLICATION

What are the enablers of instructional leadership application? What capabilities do school principals need so that they can act effectively as instructional leaders in their schools? Although the available literature on instructional leadership is quite extensive, not much is understood about principals' prerequisite qualities for engaging confidently in best instructional leadership practices.

By far, the most prominent capability deemed essential for instructional leadership application that has been accentuated in the existing literature is principals' relevant knowledge related to teaching and learning. Many activities expected of an instructional leader would be virtually impossible without the principal's own knowledge of how to create and facilitate such effective teaching and learning environments for all students. Such knowledge-driven activities aiming to promote improved teaching methods and student achievements may include those such as setting instructional goals, having a dialogue with teachers about the quality of teaching, and monitoring what is being taught, when, and how.

A helpful starting point for elaborating further details about which components of principals' knowledge may serve as enablers for instructional leadership is Shulman's (1987) typology for identifying the knowledge base needed for effective teaching. This typology developed for teachers can be applied to school principals too, because an instructional leadership approach necessitates that principals possess considerable knowledge about the core activities of schooling—teaching and learning—to support students' attainment of academic success.

This widely utilized typology (Shulman, 1987) included seven categories for teachers: (1) *Content Knowledge* refers to the knowledge teachers have about the subject matter they are teaching, such as math, chemistry, or English literature. (2) *General Pedagogical Knowledge* involves the principles of classroom management and knowledge about teaching, learning, and assessment processes. (3) *Curriculum Knowledge* refers to a broad understanding of school subjects and learning processes as manifested in standard curricula at different grade levels. (4) *Pedagogical Content Knowledge* combines the content knowledge of a particular subject and the pedagogical knowledge for teaching that particular subject. (5) *Knowledge of Learners and Their Characteristics* involves understanding of how students' characteristics may affect their learning. (6) *Knowledge of Educational Contexts* refers to external influencing factors, such as parents, superintendents, and the local community. (7) *Knowledge of Educational Ends* refers to normative and theoretical knowledge about the goals and values of education.

The fourth category, *Pedagogical Content Knowledge*, may be seen as Shulman's most notable innovation. According to Shulman (1986, p. 9), *Pedagogical Content Knowledge* "goes beyond knowledge of subject matter per se to the dimension of subject matter knowledge *for teaching*." This category includes: "the most useful forms of representation of those ideas, the most powerful analogies, illustrations, examples, explanations, and demonstrations—in a word, the ways of representing and formulating the subject that make it comprehensible to others" as well as "an understanding of what makes the learning of specific topics easy or difficult: the conceptions and preconceptions that students of different ages and backgrounds bring with them to the learning."

Claiming that instructional leadership application requires extensive knowledge in teaching and learning, Spillane and Louis (2002) saw Shulman's categories as applicable not only to teachers but also to instructional leaders. However, they only mentioned five of Shulman's seven categories (p. 97):

> Without an understanding of the knowledge necessary for teachers to teach well—content knowledge, general pedagogical knowledge, content specific pedagogical knowledge, curricular knowledge and knowledge of learners—school leaders will be unable to perform essential school improvement functions such as monitoring instruction and supporting teacher development.

Spillane and Louis did not explain why they omitted Shulman's last two categories: *Knowledge of Educational Contexts* and *Knowledge of Educational Ends*. Perhaps they asserted that proficiency in these categories, in which principals are usually versed, is not sufficient for instructional leadership, whereas the first five categories are more needed.

Further developing Shulman's typology for school principals, Stein and Nelson (2003) coined the term *Leadership Content Knowledge*. For them, *Leadership Content Knowledge* for school leaders is analogous to *Pedagogical Content Knowledge* for teachers. Stein and Nelson defined *Leadership Content Knowledge* as "that knowledge of subjects and how students learn them that is used by administrators when they function as instructional leaders" (p. 445). According to Stein and Nelson (p. 423):

> All administrators have solid mastery of at least one subject (and the learning and teaching of it) and . . . they develop expertise in other subjects by postholing, that is, conducting in-depth explorations of an important but bounded slice of the subject, how it is learned, and how it is taught.

Thus, the notion of *Leadership Content Knowledge* expresses an expectation from principals to dig deeply into each of the various disciplinary domains that make up the school curriculum. It could be argued that the image of a principal who has in-depth proficiency of content and pedagogy in all areas taught on campus is an unrealistic one that ignores the distributed nature of school leadership.

However, proponents of *Leadership Content Knowledge* believe that dwelling only on the impossibility of this task allows principals to shirk responsibility for building any degree of knowledge, leaving them underprepared to meet the variety of needs experienced by the diverse teachers in their schools (Brazer & Bauer, 2013). Principals who build *Leadership Content Knowledge* over time gain access to a more complete set of supervisory roles and therefore can better support teaching improvement (Quebec Fuentes & Jimerson, 2019, 2020).

To more comprehensively investigate school principals' perceptions about the relevance of Shulman's seven categories to the knowledge needed by instructional leaders, I recently undertook a qualitative empirical study (Shaked, in press). In this research, interviewed principals' statements were classified according to Shulman's seven knowledge categories, as described next.

(1) Content Knowledge

Overall, the interviewed principals in my study considered content knowledge—deep familiarity with specific academic subject matters like language, mathematics, and science—to be absolutely necessary for teachers but not essential for themselves as instructional leaders. For example, Deborah, with six years of experience as an elementary school principal, claimed that a principal "can't be as familiar with all the subjects taught in the school as the teachers are, and I do not see that as a problem." Thus, although school principals expected their teachers to exhibit mastery of the academic domains that they would need to teach their students, the principals did not attach importance to their own deep knowledge of the content materials being taught in their school. Jacob, with 11 years of experience as a high school principal, asserted: "As a principal who strives to improve the quality of teaching, I do not see any difference between areas in which I have solid mastery and those in which I do not."

Principals felt that their limited content knowledge did not impair their ability to observe classes, give meaningful feedback, and evaluate teaching. With seven years of experience as an elementary school principal, Brian explained: "Even if I am not versed in the subject that the teacher teaches, I have no problem recognizing whether the teacher herself understands the subject matter properly or not."

Martha, with 12 years of experience as a high school principal, related that even a foreign language was not an obstacle: "I observed an Arabic lesson, given in Arabic, and did not understand a word of what was said in the lesson. I had no problem giving the teacher feedback, which contributed greatly to improving the quality of her teaching."

(2) General Pedagogical Knowledge

In contrast to their perceptions about content knowledge, principals perceived their general pedagogical knowledge as an important resource in their work with teachers on improving the quality of teaching. Laura, with five years of experience as a junior high school principal, noted: "There is an array of educational principles that go beyond the specific subject matter. I am well acquainted with many such principles, and that's basically what matters."

Many interviewed principals specifically mentioned their pedagogical knowledge regarding how to obtain and maintain student collaboration with learning activities. Karen, with two years of experience as a high school principal, reported that she explained to struggling teachers how to "present work in an interesting and motivating way."

Esther, with 15 years of experience as an elementary school principal, related that she explained during a teachers' meeting "how to encourage students to raise expectations of themselves." With 19 years of experience as an elementary school principal, Beverly made clear "how to provide the conditions that will enable students to understand the work."

Principals also mentioned their proficiency in teaching methods, giving examples of how they conveyed this pedagogical knowledge to the teachers in their schools. For instance, viewing many teaching methods as cross-disciplinary and thereby appropriate for a wide range of knowledge areas, Christopher, with 18 years of experience as an elementary school principal, gave teachers an explanation of "how to introduce the lesson topic."

Sandra, with four years of experience as an elementary school principal, explained to beginning teachers "how to conduct question and answer sessions." In addition, principals shared with teachers their experience in addressing classroom discipline problems, including "creating a relaxed and fun atmosphere in the classroom" (Monica, with 19 years of experience as a high school principal) and "maintaining classroom control" (Phyllis, with two years of experience as a high school principal).

(3) Curriculum Knowledge

Principals stressed the significance of curriculum management as part of their instructional leadership role, but they did not attach much importance to in-depth familiarity with the standard curricula mandated for the various fields of knowledge. Kim, with 16 years of experience as an elementary school principal, related: "When teachers have a dilemma about the curriculum, they turn to the head of the department and, if necessary, also to an external consultant. I don't know how to give them an answer on this matter, beyond common sense."

Daniel, with 31 years of experience as an elementary school principal, clarified: "I often participate in discussions about the curricula, so I get to know them. However, those who really need to get to know them are the department heads."

Regarding the issue of curriculum, Irene (14 years of experience) shared that her junior high school aspired to create a continuous curriculum applicable to all age levels. Yet, for this purpose, she did not seek an in-depth understanding of the curriculum for herself. Instead, she elucidated: "What's important to me is that I can get the teachers together. They need to talk to each other and adjust their curricula to each other."

Similarly, Richard, with 15 years of experience as an elementary school principal, focused on coordinating the school's curriculum with teachers' modes of instruction in class on the one hand and with assessments of student learning on the other. He argued: "To coordinate curriculum, instruction, and assessment, I do not need a deep understanding of the curriculum. I need to know how to conduct a discussion, lead a process, and make decisions."

(4) Pedagogical Content Knowledge/Leadership Content Knowledge

School principals' perceptions about the relevance of pedagogical content knowledge to their instructional leadership role resembled their perceptions about content knowledge. Thus, when principals identified a need to expand pedagogical content knowledge—the understanding of how to best teach specific subject matters—they reported that they simply would turn to internal or external agents for that expertise.

Matthew, with 16 years of experience as a high school principal, saw the head of the department (e.g., the foreign language coordinator or the physics coordinator) as primarily responsible for the area of pedagogical content knowledge: "She knows her field very well and knows the particular way a teacher can teach a particular subject to a particular group of students."

Janice, with two years of experience as a high school principal, encouraged teachers to help each other in improving pedagogical content knowledge: "I focus on creating conditions within schools that enable teachers to work together and help those who do not know how to teach the subject." Philip, with 14 years of experience as an elementary school principal, described himself as "pooling resources and bringing in an external consultant who helps the teachers improve their teaching."

For themselves, principals saw no need to delve into pedagogical content knowledge, as illustrated by Elaine, with seven years of experience as a junior high school principal: "A principal has to be an intelligent person, who shows interest in many areas; however, she should primarily lead instructional processes and not necessarily know how to teach each of the areas of knowledge."

Moreover, familiarity with the pedagogical content knowledge of all the areas studied at school seemed to the principals to be an unreasonable expectation. James, with eight years of experience as an elementary school principal, asserted that "school leaders cannot know everything about teaching in the individual content areas." Similarly, Joan, with 15 years of experience as a high school principal, claimed that "the principal is not omnipotent and is unable to become acquainted with the teaching methods for all the disciplines."

As aforementioned, Leadership Content Knowledge (Stein & Nelson, 2003) is the Pedagogical Content Knowledge that is needed for school leaders. When principals did not ascribe much importance to Pedagogical Content Knowledge, they actually saw no real need for broad Leadership Content Knowledge. Leadership Content Knowledge was viewed as less critical than other areas of knowledge and as a matter to be distributed to internal and external experts.

(5) Knowledge of Learners and Their Characteristics

Principals attributed importance to this category of knowledge as an enabler for instructional leaders. They described themselves as relying on their familiarity with broader patterns of child development, group dynamics, and academic heterogeneity in order to help their teachers understand challenging students.

For example, Anthony, with 16 years of experience as a junior high school principal, helped one of his teachers understand a student who "drove her crazy" because this teenager was "arguing simply to argue." Exploring adolescent identity tasks with her, Anthony suggested that perhaps this teenager was "trying to establish his identity by resisting those in positions of authority."

In another example, Carol, with 11 years of experience as a junior high school principal, gave a teacher practical advice about a student who "always needs to be ranked highest in the class hierarchy." Utilizing her knowledge about natural reinforcements of behavior, Carol recommended that the teacher not let herself "get dragged into a power struggle with this 'alpha' student" but rather that she "give him a clear choice of whether or not to do the work and deal with the consequences."

Regarding this aspect of knowledge needed for instructional leaders, principals reported that such knowledge enabled them to help teachers understand the characteristics not only of individual students but also of the class as a whole. For instance, Kate, with eight years of experience as an elementary school principal, assisted her teachers to step back and look at the impact of the class dynamics on teaching: "In a meeting we held about this class, I explained that in such an energetic class, slow-paced teaching is impossible. You must propel the class forward."

Principals' knowledge about learner characteristics also enabled them to ensure that teachers had an awareness of student diversity "in terms of their abilities, interests, and responses to various situations" (Kimberly, with two years of experience as an elementary school principal). From a social justice perspective, Charles, with five years of experience as a high school principal, said, "Some teachers have stereotypical beliefs about poor and minority students. I believe that getting to know the students' background and its implications helps teachers to develop a multicultural mindset."

(6) Knowledge of Educational Contexts

Principals did often report utilizing their knowledge of the school's external context to enable improvements in teaching and learning. For example, they felt they understood the overseeing superintendents' expectations better than teachers did. Anne, with 11 years of experience as an elementary school principal, shared: "We attend conferences and principals' meetings and understand exactly what the district's current emphases are. Our job is to bring the latest information to the school and explain to teachers what today's expectations are."

The information that principals brought to their schools was about a wide range of instructional topics, such as preparations for national tests, policies for students with special needs, and new curricula and standards. Principals also mentioned that, in meetings with their colleagues, they heard about educational endeavors being implemented at other schools in their city, and they consequently imported such ideas into their own schools.

Based on relationships with their local community, principals identified opportunities for instructional collaborations with museums, galleries, parks, sports centers, archaeological sites, tourist attractions, libraries, experts from various fields, and more. Principals also helped teachers understand what parents wanted.

Patrick, with three years of experience as an elementary school principal, argued that because of his extensive relationship with students' parents, he better understands their priorities: "I instructed the teachers to reduce the amount of homework because I realized that, from the parents' point of view, we are exaggerating." Similarly, Dorothy, with four years of experience as an elementary school principal, urged teachers to regularly distribute academic updates to families because "even if it doesn't seem very important to teachers, I know how much the parents appreciate it."

(7) Knowledge of Educational Ends

Principals considered their understanding of educational goals to be very relevant to their role as instructional leaders. They believed that setting instructional goals required seeing the big picture of the school, and they, as principals, were better equipped than the teachers for this. "I know better than teachers exactly what the status of our school is in the national exams, so I help them define the goals that we must strive to achieve," stated Michelle, with 14 years of experience as a high school principal.

Principals also mentioned their up-to-date knowledge in education: "I know better than most teachers what the latest trends in education are. I set the teaching objectives of the school accordingly," said Ruth, with 14 years of experience as an elementary school principal. In addition, principals claimed that setting clear and measurable goals is "a matter of training." "I deal with it all the time, so I am much more skilled at it than the teachers," asserted Sharon, with eight years of experience as an elementary school principal.

To guide teachers in setting instructional goals, principals relied not only on data or information but also on their values. With 13 years of experience as a high school principal, Crystal was a social justice leader: "I'm not sure all my teachers see the importance in creating a learning climate that provides all students with equal opportunities regardless of race, class, gender, and other characteristics." However, "as long as I'm the principal here, it's binding on everyone." Like other principals, Crystal believed that her own priorities obligated all teachers in her school.

CONCLUSION

The findings of my study (Shaked, in press), which explored principals' perceptions regarding the kinds of knowledge required in order to effectively apply instructional leadership, showed that principals ascribed much importance to *General Pedagogical Knowledge* and *Knowledge of Learners and Their Characteristics*, perceiving these two areas of cross-curricular knowledge as enabling them to guide, supervise, and evaluate teachers. Particularly, their *General Pedagogical Knowledge*, which answers the question of how, in general, to teach and manage a classroom effectively, allowed principals to observe classes and provide meaningful feedback.

In addition, *Knowledge of Learners and Their Characteristics* enabled principals to help teachers deal with challenging students. Beyond these two categories, principals also saw themselves as making a unique contribution to better teaching and learning due to their *Knowledge of Educational Contexts* and *Knowledge of Educational Ends*.

Viewing themselves as standing between the extra- and intra-school worlds, they utilized their *Knowledge of Educational Contexts* to bring innovative instructional knowledge from the school's local environment into the school and to establish collaborations (see Chapter 12). Also, seeing themselves as more familiar with educational objectives compared to teachers, principals used their *Knowledge of Educational Ends* to set the school's instructional goals.

On the other hand, the subject-specific areas of knowledge were considered by principals as less necessary for instructional leadership application, including *Content Knowledge*, *Pedagogical Content Knowledge*, and *Curriculum Knowledge*. From principals' perspective, they cannot and should not need to obtain in-depth knowledge of all the different content areas. For them, these areas of responsibility should be distributed to department heads, with the help of external consultants.

In other words, principals expressed the belief that in their role as instructional leader, they do not have to give fine-grain guidance and direction to each of the disciplines taught in the school. Instead, they need to know how to manage the instructional program by leading instructional processes and making instructional decisions in various content areas, based on their cross-curricular knowledge of teaching and learning.

Moreover, principals viewed department heads, not themselves, as needing broad content knowledge. Believing that "nobody can do it all," principals considered that any expectation for them to have a full, comprehensive understanding of all subject matters and their pedagogies and curricula on campus would be unreasonable. Furthermore, from principals' perspective, such deep "super-heroic" mastery of all the areas taught in the school is, in fact, unnecessary because effective instructional leadership is by definition not a one-person job.

Distributing instructional leadership does not mean that the principal delegates responsibility to others and then remains aloof from what is happening in the classrooms. Rather, principals perceived their instructional leadership application as mobilizing teacher leaders, ensuring that they obtain the relevant fine-grain knowledge, and providing ongoing support for their team.

PRACTICAL RECOMMENDATIONS ON THE KNOWLEDGE ENABLING INSTRUCTIONAL LEADERSHIP APPLICATION FOR POLICYMAKERS, PRINCIPAL EDUCATORS, SUPERINTENDENTS, AND PRINCIPALS

- Principals should be selected and evaluated mainly according to their mastery of *General Pedagogical Knowledge* and *Knowledge of Learners and Their Characteristics*.
- Principals should invest ongoing efforts into acquiring up-to-date knowledge in the fields of *General Pedagogical Knowledge* and *Knowledge of Learners and Their Characteristics*.
- Principals should be encouraged to utilize their *Knowledge of Educational Contexts* and *Knowledge of Educational Ends* to inform instructional decision making.
- Principals should learn how to give feedback, evaluate teaching, and make instructional decisions in subject areas with which they have limited acquaintance.
- Principals should find experts inside and outside the school to advise them on subject-specific areas of knowledge, including *Content Knowledge*, *Pedagogical Content Knowledge*, and *Curriculum Knowledge*.
- Principals should see instructional leadership as an organizational function that extends beyond the sole position of the principal, enacting distributed instructional leadership.
- To promote willingness to take up the intimidating mantle of instructional leadership, principal educators and mentors should explicitly assure prospective or novice school leaders that they do not need fine-grain knowledge of diverse contents and curricula to act as influential instructional leaders.

REFERENCES

Brazer, S. D., & Bauer, S. C. (2013). Preparing instructional leaders: A model. *Educational Administration Quarterly, 49*(4), 645–684.

Quebec Fuentes, S., & Jimerson, J. B. (2019). Tackling instructional mismatch: Targeted intentional learning can build leaders' content knowledge. *The Learning Professional, 40*(5), 32–35.

Quebec Fuentes, S., & Jimerson, J. B. (2020). Role enactment and types of feedback: The influence of leadership content knowledge on instructional leadership efforts. *Journal of Educational Supervision, 3*(2), 6–31.

Shaked, H. (in press). Perceptions of school principals regarding the knowledge needed for instructional leadership. *Educational Management, Administration & Leadership*.

Shulman, L. (1986). Those who understand: Knowledge growth in teaching. *Educational Researcher*, *15*(2), 4–14.

Shulman, L. (1987). Knowledge and teaching: Foundations of the new reform. *Harvard Educational Review*, 57(1), 1–23.

Spillane, J. P., & Louis, K. S. (2002). School improvement process and practices: Professional learning for building instructional capacity. In J. Murphy (Ed.), *The educational leadership challenge: Redefining leadership for the 21st century* (pp. 83–104). University of Chicago.

Stein, M. K., & Nelson, B. S. (2003). Leadership content knowledge. *Educational Evaluation and Policy Analysis*, *25*(4), 423–448.

Chapter 2

Relationships Enabling Instructional Leadership Application

ABSTRACT

Principalship is inherently based on relationships, which are the cornerstone of many school leadership aspects. Particularly, the principal as an instructional leader should possess the capability to build strong, healthy relationships with various stakeholders. This chapter suggests that the basis for instructional leadership application is enabled by four intrapersonal and interpersonal relationships that principals need to cultivate: (1) with themselves; (2) with mid-level school leaders; (3) with teachers; and (4) with external stakeholders. Finally, the chapter offers practical recommendations regarding the relationships that enable the application of instructional leadership.

BUILDING POSITIVE RELATIONSHIPS FOR INSTRUCTIONAL LEADERSHIP APPLICATION

Although principals as instructional leaders are central figures in promoting high levels of academic achievement for students, their influence on students is mainly indirect—mediated by factors such as the school culture and the instructional program. The degree to which the principal dedicates attention to teaching and learning and safeguards the time allotted to improving instruction conveys these activities' importance to the staff. Principals who enact instructional leadership do so by influencing teachers' teaching strategies and priorities, which, in turn, influence student outcomes.

Thus, healthy principal-teacher relationships are an essential enabler of instructional leadership application (Robinson, 2010). Through such positive relationships, instructional leaders can engage with teachers in productive and respectful conversations about the quality of teaching and learning (Le Fevre & Robinson, 2015). Such principal-teacher relationships have been found to help teachers adopt more effective teaching practices (Alsobaie, 2015). Moreover, they have been found to significantly contribute to improving student achievements (Edgerson et al., 2006; Price, 2015). In this context, transformational leadership, which emphasizes building trust and supporting the needs of teachers, may be considered necessary but insufficient for instructional leadership (see Marks & Printy, 2003 and Bowers, 2020).

Instructional leadership emphasizes aspects of coordination and control, such as supervision, evaluation, and monitoring (see Introduction and Table 1 about the instructional program). Therefore, it may be seen as task-oriented leadership, which focuses on getting things done to achieve defined standards and meet particular goals, rather than relationship-oriented leadership, which focuses on building lasting relationships with team members and ensuring their job satisfaction.

However, the conceptual frameworks of instructional leadership (presented in the introduction above) also include relationship-oriented functions, such as leading a learning community and communicating the school's goals. Moreover, the relational nature of the school leader's role cannot be ignored. Almost every task assigned to a school principal requires some degree of relational behavior.

Therefore, the capacity to build good relationships may be seen as vital for instructional leadership application, as described in many places in this book. The role that relationships play in instructional leadership application reinforces the claim that—because leadership is multidimensional rather than dichotomous—effective instructional leaders are those who know how to integrate a focus on tasks with attention to relationships.

Particularly, instructional leadership today is perceived as more decentralized. In the past, the instructional leadership approach was considered incompatible with shared or distributed leadership. The principal was considered to be the only one coordinating and controlling the school, without significant teacher participation, using "a directive and top-down approach to school leadership" (Hallinger, 2003, p. 337).

Instructional leadership is primarily characterized by the school principal's actions that emphasize the setting of specific goals and the monitoring of teaching methods and student achievement, which are top-down authoritative types of leadership behaviors. Instructional leadership has not generally placed primary emphasis on principals' actions that focus on motivating teachers, building lasting relationships with them, and ensuring their satisfaction and general well-being. Instructional leadership thereby requires teachers to meet top-down expectations, whereas contemporary thinking is more about empowerment, developmental cultures, and learning organizations.

In this context, instructional leadership is contrasted with transformational leadership, where principals lead changes based on their ability to inspire teachers and encourage them to build a community of practitioners in the school. However, eventually, instructional leadership was recognized as an approach requiring skillsets that typically go beyond those possessed by any one individual in the school and requiring allotments of time that surpass what one principal could accomplish alone (see also in the previous chapter, which showed a deep reliance by instructional leaders on department heads and external experts).

Therefore, it became clear that instructional leadership application cannot be a solo performance: "It is essential to reformulate instructional leadership both as a collective identity and in terms of a set of shared functional responsibilities" (Hallinger & Murphy, 2013, p. 16). As long as instructional leadership's aim is made possible by working together with school stakeholders toward that common goal of improving teaching and learning, its application does not have to be based on an authoritative, top-down approach.

Principals' application of instructional leadership in a distributed manner highlights the importance of the relationships inherent to its success. Special status in distributed instructional leadership is given to teachers serving as mid-level school leaders, who have management responsibility for a team of teachers or an aspect of the school's work. These teachers, who are the driving force behind improving the quality of teaching and learning, have a relationship with the school principal that is different from that of the schoolroom teachers.

Moreover, principals focus not only on activities taking place within the school but also on importing the resources, support, and knowledge from outside the school that are needed to improve academic results. Thus, in addition to their intra-school relationships, instructional leaders also cultivate good relationships with various stakeholders from the extra-school world.

To further explore these various relationships involved in instructional leadership application, I interviewed school leaders in a recent study (Shaked, in press). Qualitative data analysis from this study revealed that instructional leadership application does not only involve principal-teacher relationships. In fact, four different relationships were identified as enablers of instructional leadership application: (1) principals' relationship with themselves; (2) principals' relationship with mid-level school leaders; (3) principals' relationship with teachers; and (4) principals' relationship with external stakeholders, as presented next.

Principals' Relationship with Themselves

The first relationship enabling application of instructional leadership is principals' relationship with themselves. A healthy relationship with oneself—acknowledging one's own strengths, weaknesses, desires, and concerns—enables the principal to engage effectively in the other important relationships required for instructional leadership application.

The interviewed principals in my study (Shaked, in press) emphasized the importance of self-awareness, referring to an inwardly focused evaluative process in which individuals develop a better understanding of their own character, feelings, motives, and desires. Lisa, with 12 years of experience as a high school principal, said her awareness of her own weaknesses allowed her to be less critical of teachers' work: "I know I make mistakes too, and I'm not perfect either, so I do not expect my teachers to be perfect, even when I criticize their work." Lisa's self-awareness made her humbler, and therefore also more forgiving.

David, with three years of experience as an elementary school principal, also utilized his self-awareness to make it easier for teachers to accept criticism of their work: "I tell them of my own quirks so that no one feels hurt. I explain to teachers that part of my criticism is because of my own 'pet peeves,' which aren't necessarily the most critical components of quality teaching."

David was not only aware of the influence of his "quirks" on his reactions but also shared his self-awareness with the teachers, thereby modeling to them that each person can have individual preferences regarding quality teaching but should learn to know their own idiosyncrasies. To be noted, the latter two examples may perhaps also be seen as reflecting these principals' attempts to address significant critiques of instructional leadership concerning its authoritative top-down nature and to bypass power distance (see Chapter 6).

With 11 years of experience as an elementary school principal, Anne talked about self-awareness of hidden biases in the context of hiring new teachers. She said honestly: "I used to have many biases about teaching candidates. I formed a negative opinion of one candidate because she was a single mother, or of another because he spoke with an accent that I thought seemed unintelligent, or even because someone was overweight." She recounted: "I went through a process of rooting out prejudice, which was not easy." Anne's self-awareness and self-change allowed her to make better, more bias-free decisions about teaching candidates.

Principals also mentioned that self-regulation, referring to the ability to monitor and manage emotions, thoughts, and behaviors in ways that produce positive results, is needed for instructional leadership application. Karen, with two years of experience as a high school principal, said: "When a teacher does not submit student achievement mapping or term grades on time, it really annoys me, but I know how to avoid an impulsive reaction, which can be really counterproductive." Karen's self-regulation helped her respond more effectively to teachers' failures. Similarly, self-discipline, referring to the ability to push oneself forward constantly, was also perceived by principals as necessary for instructional leadership application.

With six years of experience as an elementary school principal, Deborah did not despair when the academic results of her school declined: "I encouraged myself. I talked to someone I trusted, venting my frustrations, and reminded myself that it was temporary. I knew for sure that I could improve our results if I put in the effort to do so." Deborah not only remained motivated but also showed compassion for herself, rather than being overly self-critical.

Principals' Relationship with Mid-Level School Leaders

In addition to the intrapersonal aspect described above, several interpersonal relationships appear to enable instructional leadership application. The first to be discussed here is the principal's relationships with mid-level school leaders. Considering that mid-level leaders play a critical role in leading teams of teachers to ensure that curricula are developed, delivered, and reviewed, that programs are assessed, and that teachers are evaluated, the principal's good relationship with them is a necessary condition for leading instructional improvement processes in the school.

Principals in my study (Shaked, in press) viewed their mid-level leaders to be their prominent supporters. Therefore, the principals shared planned changes or decisions with the school's mid-level leaders before discussing them with other teachers. For example, James, with eight years of experience as an elementary school principal, said: "When I set new standards for teaching and learning in school, it can elicit some resistance. That's why I first persuade the circle closest to me—the grade-level heads and department heads—so that they will support me later."

Principals expected their mid-level school leaders to support them when conveying learning requirements during formal and informal teacher discussions, as clarified by Alexander, with 11 years of experience as an elementary school principal: "I don't want to stand alone in front of all the teachers. I want there to be more voices to support my side, and to me, that's exactly the role of mid-level leaders."

Some principals revealed that they actually viewed their mid-level leaders as secret partners. Esther, with 15 years of experience as an elementary school principal, told only her mid-level leaders about their district's critique of the school's achievement level: "Our superintendent said she was not happy with our results on the national tests. I did not tell all the teachers about it, but I did share it with the management team members." Ruth, with 14 years of experience as an elementary school principal, told a relevant mid-level leader about her plan to fire a pedagogically weak teacher: "It's important for me to know what the grade-level coordinator thinks, and I trust her not to reveal my plans to those who do not need to know about them."

Principals also often saw the mid-level leaders as close friends. With 14 years of experience as a high school principal, Michelle explained: "I don't go to the family celebrations of all the teachers in the school, but I do go to the events of the mid-level leaders because they are the people closest to me." The principals mentioned mainly formal mid-level leaders, who have a defined responsibility for a field of knowledge, a group of teachers, or an aspect of the school's work.

However, they also mentioned relationships with informal mid-level leaders—teachers who do not hold an official role in the school but who are valued both by the management team and by the teaching staff and therefore have an influence in the school. For example, George, with 16 years of experience as an elementary school principal, described one such mid-level leader in his school: "She doesn't hold any formal position, but I really appreciate her experience and wisdom, so I keep in touch with her continuously to hear her opinion on the instructional topics at hand."

Principals' Relationship with Teachers

A major relationship required for instructional leadership application, of course, is that of the principal with the teachers. Instructional leadership practices—which ultimately target the teachers' behavior in classrooms—are not feasible without a healthy principal-teacher relationship.

A good relationship with teachers—including characteristics such as open communication, mutual respect, and trust—is required, first and foremost, to mobilize teachers' support for the school's identified instructional goals. Sandra, with four years of experience as an elementary school principal, explained: "I can wave a flag of pedagogical goals, and find that no one is following me. If I am not connected to the teachers, I will be left standing alone with my goals."

Good relationships also reduce opposition to new instructional initiatives, as expressed by Patricia, a junior high school principal with 14 years of experience: "When there is a good relationship between the teachers and me, they are much less opposed to new programs and new ideas that I bring up."

A good relationship with teachers creates a balance with the need to supervise those teachers' practice, as Bob, with 16 years of experience as a high school principal, explained: "Observations and conversations with teachers about the quality of their practice naturally create tension. To complement this, it is important to have a good relationship with them."

Similarly, Laura, with five years of experience as a junior high school principal, argued: "I have to evaluate teachers, and I don't want it to spoil my relationship with them. So I find opportunities to show them that we are also in a good relationship."

Moreover, positive principal-teacher relationships are necessary to enable a fruitful discourse on the methods used by teachers. With 16 years of experience as an elementary school principal, John claimed: "If you are not respectful and supportive, they will not agree to learn from you."

Margaret, with two years of experience as an elementary school principal, saw good relationships as a prerequisite to openness: "If my relationship with a teacher is not good, she will not be honest with me about her difficulties. A teacher who feels the need to defend herself does not share her weaknesses." Also, a good relationship with the principal increases teachers' motivation to improve their teaching quality.

Elizabeth, with two years of experience as an elementary school principal, argued that there is a reasonably broad congruence between a teacher's feeling toward the principal and her feeling toward the school: "The centrality of the principal in the school means that if, as a teacher, you get along well with her, then you'll feel good in school and will be committed to doing your job properly, and vice versa."

Principals mentioned both their relationship with all teachers as a group and their relationship with each teacher individually. From the interviewees' point of view, the principal should cultivate the relationship with the entire teaching staff as a whole, while paying special attention to teachers who have a unique need or difficulty: "I invest in cultivating my relationship with each of the teachers, but I also know how to invest especially in a teacher who for some reason needs special attention" (Alice, with 19 years of experience as an elementary school principal).

Although overly close relationships with teachers may inhibit instructional leadership application (as discussed often later in this book), positive principal-teacher relationships are crucial. These relationships, which are among the cornerstones of school leadership, may enable the principal to improve teaching practices and therefore promote student learning and success.

Principals' Relationship with External Stakeholders

Instructional leadership application requires not only good relationships with staff inside the school—mid-level leaders and other teachers, as mentioned above—but also with stakeholders from the outside-school world. To ensure instructional improvement and success, the principal must create healthy relationships with various external agents who influence the school's instructional functions.

Importantly, the principals interviewed in my study believed that good relationships with parents enable principals to mobilize support for the school's instructional goals. For example, while Monica, a high school principal with 19 years of experience, prioritized learning and academic success, the parents of some of the students at her school did not have the same opinion: "What matters most to them is that their children be happy." These parents wanted to reduce their children's amount of homework, number of exams, and workload in school. Monica claimed that "only thanks to my good relationship with them was I able to explain to them that it is impossible to achieve the happiness of their children without studying at a high level."

Michael, with seven years of experience as an elementary school principal, emphasized his good relationships with the school parents' committee: "I have built an excellent relationship with the members of the school's parents' committee. Thus I obtain legitimacy for all my instructional programs."

Good relationships with principals of other schools allowed school leaders to gather information about teaching methods, learning materials, and related issues. Speaking about colleagues in her city, Carol, with 11 years of experience as a junior high school principal, said: "Although we compete with each other for students, we are also good friends and share ideas and initiatives that may enhance our accomplishments."

Similarly, close relationships with other school principals made it possible for Jennifer, with 12 years of experience as an elementary school principal, to gather information about teaching candidates: "I'm in close contact with quite a few principals, so when I ask them about the teaching quality of teachers I want to hire, I know they will tell me the truth."

Another important set of extra-school relationships for the principal is with local municipal officials. For example, such relationships helped Philip, with 14 years of experience as an elementary school principal, to raise resources for instructional initiatives: "To implement new instructional programs, we need a budget. I have become the best friend of the person in charge of the local municipal budget, and then I can get almost anything I want from him."

Generally speaking, good extra-school relationships were seen by principals as a critical capability needed when seeking financial support for instructional enterprises. With 15 years of experience as a high school principal, Gloria said: "Fundraising is ultimately very much based on a personal relationship. No matter how great the instructional idea you have, if you do not create a connection with the person you are meeting, they won't help you."

CONCLUSION

This chapter shows that a wide range of healthy relationships is essential to enable instructional leadership application. Principals' relationship with themselves, including self-awareness, self-regulation, and self-discipline, supports their instructional leadership practices by enabling the successful formation of other necessary relationships. In addition, principals as instructional leaders attach particular importance to their relationship with the school's mid-level leaders, seeing them as the first circle of influence, which helps to lead the entire team in improving teaching and learning. This allows for a distributed approach to instructional leadership, in which talented teachers are empowered to take on leading roles, assume responsibility, and act independently.

Of course, the importance of a healthy relationship with teachers for instructional leadership application is evident from the fact that leadership is, by definition, a reciprocal leader-followers process, in which both the leader and the followers play an active role in the relationship. Through such a positive relationship, instructional leaders can involve teachers in achieving the school's instructional goals and engage with them in productive and respectful conversations about the quality of teaching and learning.

Finally, instructional leadership application involves not only an internal focus but also a significant outward focus. Thus, instructional leaders not only concentrate on teaching, learning, and assessment activities taking place within the school but also on building positive relationships with parents, officials, colleagues from other schools, and additional external stakeholders.

Such relations are necessary to explain the school's instructional mission to various stakeholders, create partnerships that help student learning, search for external innovative instructional knowledge, and mobilize support and funding for instructional programs from outside the school. In sum, the personal capability of the principal to establish a range of positive relationships is a prerequisite for the successful application of instructional leadership.

PRACTICAL RECOMMENDATIONS ON RELATIONSHIPS ENABLING INSTRUCTIONAL LEADERSHIP APPLICATION FOR POLICYMAKERS, PRINCIPAL EDUCATORS, SUPERINTENDENTS, AND PRINCIPALS

- Principals should develop their self-awareness through both external feedback and introspection toward their experiences, emotional triggers, strengths, and weaknesses.
- Principals should learn the basics of interpersonal relationships, including providing and receiving feedback, welcoming diversity, and communicating.
- Principals should cultivate their relationships with mid-level leaders so that they will support the instructional work of the principal and help achieve the school's instructional goals.
- Principals should establish supportive relationships with teachers by means such as listening, caring, appreciating, and being available and visible.
- Principals should foster healthy relationships with the parents of their students and seek out opportunities to cooperate with them.
- Principals should create close relationships with other principals, even if their schools compete for the same students.
- Principals should embrace opportunities to build lasting relationships with those who can provide resources that will be used to achieve the school's pedagogical goals.

REFERENCES

Alsobaie, M. F. (2015). The principal's relationship with teacher and development literacy of elementary school students. *Journal of Education and Practice*, 6(35), 149–155.

Bowers, A. J. (2020). *Examining a congruency-typology model of leadership for learning using two-level latent class analysis with TALIS 2018*. OECD Publishing.

Edgerson, D. E., Kritsonis, W. A., & Herrington, D. (2006). *The critical role of the teacher-principal relationship in the improvement of student achievement in public schools of the United States*. http://files.eric.ed.gov/fulltext/ED491985.pdf

Hallinger, P. (2003). Leading educational change: Reflections on the practice of instructional and transformational leadership. *Cambridge Journal of Education*, 33(3), 329–352.

Hallinger, P., & Murphy, J. F. (2013). Running on empty? Finding the time and capacity to lead learning. *Bulletin of the National Association of Secondary School Principals*, 97(1), 5–21.

Le Fevre, D. M., & Robinson, V. M. J. (2015). The interpersonal challenges of instructional leadership: Principals' effectiveness in conversations about performance issues. *Educational Administration Quarterly, 51*(1), 58–95.

Marks, H. M., & Printy, S. M. (2003). Principal leadership and school performance: An integration of transformational and instructional leadership. *Educational Administration Quarterly, 39*(3), 370–397.

Price, H. E. (2015). Principals' social interactions with teachers: How principal-teacher social relations correlate with teachers' perceptions of student engagement. *Journal of Educational Administration, 53*(1), 116–139.

Robinson, V. M. J. (2010). From instructional leadership to leadership capabilities: Empirical findings and methodological challenges. *Leadership and Policy in Schools, 9*(1), 1–26.

Shaked, H. (in press). Relationship-based instructional leadership. *International Journal of Leadership in Education.*

Chapter 3

Systems Thinking as an Enabler of Instructional Leadership Application

ABSTRACT

Systems thinking puts the study of wholes before that of parts. It does not try to break systems down into parts to understand them; it concentrates attention instead on how the parts act together in networks of interaction. As instructional leadership involves attempts to understand and improve complex systems, this chapter presents systems thinking as a possible enabler of instructional leaders, claiming that it contributes to the following three areas of instructional leadership: (1) improvement of the school curriculum; (2) development of professional learning communities; and (3) interpretation of performance data. The chapter ends with practicable recommendations about systems thinking as an enabler of instructional leadership application.

CONCEPTUALIZING SYSTEMS THINKING

In addition to the relevant knowledge and relationships discussed in the previous chapters as enablers of instructional leadership application, another vital capability needed for instructional leadership application is complex problem solving. Robinson (2010) proposed a model of the interrelations among three of these leadership capabilities required for instructional leaders: (a) using deep leadership content knowledge to (b) solve complex school-based problems while (c) building relational trust with staff, parents, and students.

It should be noted that Brenninkmeyer and Spillane (2008) did not succeed in directly linking differences in principals' problem-solving with differences in instructional leadership practices and student outcomes. However, Robinson (2010, p. 15) claimed that "While the links between capability in problem-solving, leadership practices, and student outcomes have been suggested rather than convincingly demonstrated, an additional case can be made from the theoretical and empirical research on problem-solving."

I propose that the concept of problem solving may be replaced with the concept of "systems thinking," which I believe is an enabler of instructional leadership application. In my study with colleagues (Shaked et al., 2018), principals' systems thinking was found to correlate significantly with instructional leadership. This chapter aims to explain how systems thinking can serve as an important enabler of instructional leadership application.

Systems thinking is considered to be an effective means for facing real-life situations. Thus, it has been proposed as a way of assisting managers to deal effectively with contemporary challenges, which often arise in richly interconnected problem situations. School leaders who face today's educational leadership complexities are among those who could benefit from systems thinking. Taking account of the fact that school principals' instructional leadership application necessitates seeing the whole picture and discovering the connections between various school elements, the current chapter describes this type of thinking and presents the results of our research (Shaked & Schechter, 2016) exploring principals' perceptions about how systems thinking may contribute to instructional leadership application.

Systems thinking stands in direct contrast to the reductionist approach espoused by René Descartes (1985), who lived in the 17th century. Reductionism attempts to understand systems by reducing them to their simpler parts. According to this reductionist approach, the answer to every "what is this" question would always be "this is what it is made of." Thus, entities of a given kind are considered to be collections or combinations of entities of a more basic kind. Therefore, the best reductionist strategy for grasping a complex phenomenon is to attempt to provide an explanation of it in terms of ever-smaller entities.

In contrast to the reductionist approach, systems thinking is a holistic perspective, which believes that everything is connected to everything else. Thus, the only way to fully understand a system is to understand its parts in relation to the whole. While for the reductionists "the simple is the source of the complex," for systems thinkers "the whole is more than the sum of its parts." Here are some of the definitions and explanations for systems thinking formulated by scholars in recent decades. Senge (1990, p. 68) defined systems thinking as:

a discipline for seeing wholes. It is a framework for seeing interrelationships rather than things, for seeing patterns of change rather than static "snapshots." It is a set of general principles. . . . It is also a set of specific tools and techniques.

Thus, Senge conceptualized this type of thinking as a conceptual framework but also as a set of practical devices. With regard to the complex ability for inferring about systems, Richmond (1994) claimed that systems thinking is "the art and science of making reliable inferences about behavior by developing an increasingly deep understanding of underlying structure" (p. 141). Checkland (1999, p. 318) asserted that systems thinking is:

an epistemology which, when applied to human activity, is based upon the four basic ideas: emergence, hierarchy, communication, and control as characteristics of systems. When applied to natural or designed systems, the crucial characteristic is the emergent properties of the whole.

Focusing on its practical aspects, Arnold and Wade (2015) opined that systems thinking is "a set of synergistic analytic skills used to improve the capability of identifying and understanding systems, predicting their behaviors, and devising modifications to them in order to produce desired effects. These skills work together as a system" (p. 675). Despite the absence of a commonly accepted definition for systems thinking, these diverse definitions clearly yield two main complementary meanings: rising above the separate components to see the whole system, and thinking about each separate component as a part of the whole system.

Through the lens of systems thinking, the multitude of variables existing in any system may be seen as causally related in feedback loops, which consist of the system's outputs that are routed back as inputs, as part of a circuit of causation (Senge, 1990, 2014). The feedback loops themselves interact, and these interactions constitute the structure of the system and determine its behavior.

Feedback loops challenge the commonly perceived relation between cause and effect, which considers a first event to be responsible for the occurrence of a second event. From the feedback-loop perspective, understanding the system as a whole is necessary because the first event does influence the second, but the second event also influences the first, leading to a circular series of events. Thus, causation in systems is not wholly obvious and tends not to be direct. Moreover, time may pass between an action and its result; such a delay may create a situation where one can easily underreact or overreact, because the full impact of the action cannot yet be assessed correctly.

Several researchers have demonstrated how the application of systems thinking assists managers in coping successfully with complex situations in a wide range of areas. However, systems thinking in the context of school leadership has not yet received sufficient empirical attention. In an attempt to narrow this gap for the education context, our previous study (Shaked & Schechter, 2014, 2017) described the four major ways in which school leaders apply the systems thinking view and perform at the systems thinking level:

1. The first characteristic of systems-thinking leaders is the capacity for *leading wholes*—a holistic point of view oriented toward seeing the big picture and not only its individual parts. Using systems thinking in this way enables principals to view all aspects of school life as one large system.
2. The second characteristic—*influencing indirectly*—refers to leaders' ability to address the school's tasks and challenges circuitously. This strategy is based on principals' awareness that countless reciprocal influences are at play among various school elements, each of which is connected to others, affecting them and being affected by them.
3. The third characteristic—*adopting a multidimensional view*—refers to seeing several aspects of a given issue simultaneously. Effective principals notice a wide range of reasons for a given issue's emergence and existence, take into account a variety of its consequences, and predict various options for its future development.
4. The fourth characteristic—*evaluating significance*—considers elements of school life according to their significance for the entire system. Principals distinguish between important and less important issues to be resolved, identifying patterns.

Considering that instructional leadership application requires principals to optimize the entire system as a whole, our study (Shaked & Schechter, 2016) sought to explore systems thinking as a potential contributor to principals' application of instructional leadership in their schools. As elaborated next, our research outcomes found that principals viewed systems thinking as an important enabler for the following three areas of their instructional leadership: (1) improving school curriculum; (2) developing school-based professional learning communities; and (3) using performance data.

Systems Thinking About School Curriculum

In the eyes of school principals, a major benefit of systems thinking is its holistic facilitation of the school's curriculum development. Emphasizing the importance of the whole and the interdependence of its parts, systems thinking assists school leaders in grasping the "big picture" of curriculum. This includes not only the separate curriculum components and their interrelations (for different subject matters and across grade levels) but also the interrelationships between curricula and other school issues.

The diverse principals interviewed in our study (Shaked & Schechter, 2016) highlighted that, from the systems thinking perspective, coordination is a major issue that principals must understand and address. Principals often review curricula, and they also usually review teaching practices. Obviously, they review student achievement too. However, systems thinking facilitates the coordination of these different aspects. The coordination of curriculum, instruction, and assessment reflects principals' ability to *see the whole beyond the parts*, which is one of the two main meanings of systems thinking.

Gladys, for example, with 12 years of experience as a high school principal, relayed that she focused her leadership efforts on coordinating school curriculum with teachers' modes of instruction in class and with the assessment of student learning. In her view, beyond improving each of these areas separately, the principal should make sure they fit in with each other:

- "Many things affect student achievement: The curricular programs must be well prepared, the teaching methods to be used must be updated and student-centered, and so on. However, to improve student achievements, which is the ultimate goal of all our work here, I cannot deal with each of these topics separately. Standards, curriculum, instruction, and evaluation must be combined. They're different dimensions of the same issue."

Thus, Gladys sought to coordinate three major aspects of the instructional leaders' purview: curriculum, instruction, and assessment. Moreover, consistently keeping in mind that improving student achievements was her goal and that this goal must be measured by standard-based assessments, Gladys maintained that the school's curriculum, instruction, and assessments must be aligned with the standards. Gladys's point of view reflects systems thinking, which claims that an improvement process must be holistic.

From the systems thinking perspective, improving each component separately will not result in improvement of the whole, because the whole is more than the sum of its parts. Moreover, to improve the whole, what must be optimized is mainly the interaction among its parts. Gladys implemented this perspective to enhance student achievements; she did not address each step in the process separately but rather increased the interactions among them.

Similarly, Joyce, with eight years of experience as a high school principal, believed that if there is a disconnect between standards, curriculum, instruction, and evaluation, then student achievement levels will not rise. For her, the coordination of these elements is an ongoing process because curriculum, teaching practices, and evaluations all cycle through improvements. Moreover, Joyce did not consider this task of coordinating standards, curriculum, instruction, and assessment to be exclusively her responsibility. Instead, she regarded this as an issue that should be dealt with by all teachers:

- "I established staff meetings during which teachers work together to interpret the standards, study the curriculum, share effective teaching strategies, examine benchmarks, and analyze student work. I want the teachers to see the connections between all the links of the chain, because they are all dependent on each other."

Thus, Joyce not only coordinated standards, curriculum, teaching, and assessment herself but also developed a professional peer learning community. As will be explained below, developing such a community that provides meaningful staff development may also be seen as an expression of systems thinking.

Wayne, with seven years of experience as a junior high school principal, also saw standards, curriculum, and teaching as closely intertwined with measures for assessing performance:

- "The assessment tasks are integrated within the learning-teaching-assessment process. The assessment provides performance data to teachers and students regarding their progress toward achieving the standards, and this data is used to judge the effectiveness of the curriculum and materials in use, and the effectiveness of instruction. I would say that the assessment provides us with the diagnostic information that assists us in identifying strengths and weaknesses in order to establish priorities in planning our educational work."

Systems thinking involves seeing separate events as parts of an ongoing process. Seeing teaching, learning, assessment according to standards, and improvement of curriculum and instruction as an iterative process, Wayne demonstrated using systems thinking to holistically enhance school curriculum.

The systems thinking perspective also facilitates holistic development of curriculum vertically, up and down the different age levels. For instance, the secondary school headed by Louise, who had been in the position for six years when interviewed, is divided into three units, with each two-grade level comprising a separate unit. Performing at the systems level, Louise considered the curriculum of the different units to be parts of one continual spiraling process. Thus, she expected teachers to be familiar not only with their own students' curriculum but also with the curricula for all grade levels in the school:

- "The syllabus for all age levels is cyclic, meaning that we always review the previous material when we are about to teach a new subject. The problem is that in our school there's a break between every two levels. But you are not only the teacher of your own pupils; you are a team member. Teachers should know a bit more than just what happens in their own classroom, because the curriculum is actually a continuous one across all age levels."

Louise considered the curriculum to be spiral, with material being revisited repeatedly over the years rather than learned once within a short period of time. Put differently, she did not see each grade-level's curriculum as standing on its own. Instead, she saw it holistically, demonstrating that she could *see the whole beyond the parts*, which is one of the two main meanings of systems thinking. Similarly, she implemented her systems thinking view regarding the teaching staff. Instead of seeing each teacher as working with a particular age group only, her view was holistic, regarding each teacher as one who works in the whole united entity making up the school.

In another example of systems thinking as an enabler of instructional leadership, Ryan, with five years of experience as a junior high school principal, articulated a holistic approach connecting his students' reading skills across the various disciplines comprising his school's curriculum. In junior high school, students should already have unlocked the secrets to decoding words and putting them together to read sentences and paragraphs—skills learned in elementary school. Now in junior high school, students need to acquire the comprehension skills that can permit them to delve into more sophisticated literature. For Ryan, developing such reading comprehension competencies among junior high school students should be a target not only in literature classrooms but during all other lessons as well:

- "This is the time when our students develop their advanced reading skills, which allow them to master the contents of various disciplines. Thus, developing reading comprehension skills is not a matter for language and literature lessons only. The strategies imparted in language lessons must be applied in all classes; otherwise they may be worthless."

Claiming that the skills for comprehending written texts cannot be acquired effectively by junior high school students without being exercised across all classrooms and subjects, Ryan saw dedicated reading comprehension lessons as only one part of a much broader systemic learning process. In other words, he demonstrated an important ability to *see the parts in the context of the whole*, which is one of the two main meanings of systems thinking.

In sum, principals' own voices about how they may think systemically in their everyday work suggest that systems thinking may contribute significantly to instructional leadership application by enabling principals' holistic development of the school curriculum. This holistic lens facilitates recognition of the interrelations among curricula for different disciplines and different age levels, as well as the interrelations between curricula and other important aspects of work in the school.

Systems Thinking About Professional Learning Communities

From principals' perspective, the second important area that can substantially benefit from systems thinking is the development of meaningful school-based professional learning communities, where educators collaborate to improve teaching skills and students' academic performance. As mentioned above, developing people is a key element of instructional leadership (see Introduction and Table 1). Educators who are forming a professional learning community must work together to achieve their collective purpose of quality learning for all students (DuFour et al., 2021).

To bring this collective goal to fruition, school leaders must be able to promote a collaborative atmosphere among the teachers and mid-level leaders, which can benefit from a systems thinking approach. For instance, Elizabeth, with 13 years of experience as a high school principal, proposed a conceptual basis for forming a professional learning community at school:

- "I believe that a schoolteacher is not only the teacher of her own students; she is also a part of the school team that is responsible for ensuring each and every student's learning. For this reason, I expect every professional in the school to engage with colleagues in an ongoing exploration of crucial questions that drive our work because, whether you like it or not, you are part of a joint development process that is taking place throughout the whole school."

Elizabeth regarded teachers as members of one large organization that operates as a whole, meaning that all teachers should work together to help improve the entire school. Each individual teacher should not only focus on their own position but also should feel responsible for the whole school's output, and therefore should engage in collaborative learning, sharing, and support. This point of view that considers each teacher as a part of a whole team reflects *seeing the parts in the context of the whole*, which is one of the two main meanings of systems thinking.

Edward, with 13 years of experience as an elementary school principal, also linked the idea of the professional learning community to the systems thinking framework:

- "Some teachers are so loyal to their specific jobs that they are not concerned with how their decisions impact any other teachers or classes within the school. They have little sense of responsibility for the results attained by other classes' students. I believe that, when working as a learning community, teachers will see the school as a whole interacting organization, where each decision is evaluated for how it impacts the whole."

Edward claimed that when teachers in the school focus too closely on their own positions and responsibilities, they may miss out on the bigger picture. Like Elizabeth, Edward's conceptual basis for developing a professional learning community reflects *seeing the parts in the context of the whole*, which is one of the two main meanings of systems thinking.

However, for Edward, systems thinking may also emerge as an outcome from working as a professional learning community, because when teachers are required to see not only their own job but also the purpose of the school in which they work or how they contribute to the whole, they may develop a desirable systemic perspective.

Alan, with five years of experience as a junior high school principal, also viewed the need for a professional learning community through a systemic lens:

- "In my opinion, principals should not impose their own predetermined way. They must respect various voices and work to establish a common path. They should lead from the center rather than from the top, and should concentrate on presenting core questions. I believe that joint discussion of these questions will result in better school performance."

Alan justified the establishment of a professional learning community without redefining the meaning of being a schoolteacher as Elizabeth and Edward did. Instead, he redefined the meaning of being a school principal.

According to Alan, the principal does not have to be the smartest person in the room; the kind of wisdom that the principal needs is collective, by facilitating dialogue and collaboration among the teaching staff. However, like Elizabeth and Edward, Alan's position also represented systems thinking, as he emphasized mainly the whole and the interactions between its parts.

Not only does systems thinking provide the conceptual justification for principals' establishment of professional learning communities, but it also increases school leaders' willingness to consider others' opinions. A principal who understands that each situation within the system is multifaceted and contains numerous possible implications seeks to understand the full picture by listening to varied points of view. In this context, William, with six years of experience as a junior high school principal, stated:

- "A school principal who thinks that he knows everything about teaching and learning, and that there is nothing left for him to learn, will become 'stuck' and eventually 'reach his expiration date,' becoming obsolete. Instead of operating as a 'lone ranger' and feeling like I must know it all, I get the teachers to think about school improvement together with me."

According to William, principals should refrain from thinking that they know everything about school improvement. Instead, they should constantly learn from the people around them, establishing collaborative learning. Willingness to reach decisions while taking others' opinions into account reflects *adopting a multidimensional view*, which as noted above is one of the two major characteristics of systems thinking among school leaders.

Lori, with eight years of experience as a high school principal, described how seeing the big picture encouraged the teachers at her school to participate in professional collaborative learning:

- "Teachers sometimes grumble about the many meetings and discussions in which they must participate at school. However, when I established our professional learning community, its discussion—on the broad topics related to the school's instructional goals and on the actual results of our efforts to attain them—motivated teachers to participate because it enabled them to see their own specific work in the context of the whole system. That gave meaning to their own concrete educational work, beyond their usual limited point of view."

According to Lori, the broad perspective of the whole system provides deeper meaning to the daily minutiae of the individual's work within that system. This reflects not only the principal's but also the teachers' ability to *see the parts in the context of the whole*, which is one of the two main meanings of systems thinking.

To summarize, principals' perceptions suggest that systems thinking can significantly enable instructional leadership application by facilitating the development of professional learning communities. Systems thinking provides the conceptual basis and the motivation necessary for turning the teaching staff into a collaborative, mutually enriching, and self-motivating learning community that strives to improve teaching and learning. At the same time, this way of thinking also increases the principal's willingness to consider the variety of opinions and perspectives conducive to effective collaboration.

Systems Thinking About Interpretation of Performance Data

As schools face increasing pressure to improve student achievement, the use of data has become more central to the way principals evaluate teachers' practices and monitor students' academic progress. Armed with data and the means to harness the information that data can provide, principals can make instructional changes aimed at improving student achievement, such as prioritizing instruction over other goals, refining instructional methods, and dedicating additional individual instruction time to students who are struggling with particular subjects.

Therefore, several frameworks of instructional leadership referred to the crucial role of using data (see Introduction and Table 1). Principals' perceptions suggest that systems thinking is an essential facilitator of their data analysis and evidence-based decision making.

As aforementioned, one of the characteristics of systems thinking in school leadership is *adopting a multidimensional view*. When principals consider a single occurrence at school to have several causes and therefore view a single explanation for it as unsatisfactory, they are exhibiting a multidimensional view.

John, with five years of experience as a high school principal, offered the example of a meeting intended to discuss his school's recent results on national language testing. The results were not as good as the teaching staff believed they could have been. During the discussion, some staff members claimed that they had identified a "single exclusive explanation" for these disappointing achievement levels: One teacher said that the reason was the lack of an instructional coordinator; another asserted that the school simply did not allocate a sufficient number of hours to language classes; and a third teacher maintained that the teachers are not professional enough. John criticized this reductionist way of thinking in relating this anecdote during his interview:

- "There's always somebody, or a few somebodies, who say they know the exact cause for the problem at hand. I believe there's never one single reason for anything that happens in a school, or anywhere, for that matter. A school is such a complicated entity, consisting of so many components that influence each other, that there are always quite a few reasons for anything that occurs in it. Of course, some of the reasons are primary and some are secondary. However, to improve our achievements, we must avoid pointing to one single reason for anything, because looking for such a reason without considering all the varied factors influencing student achievements makes it difficult to attain a full explanation of our results."

John was capable of juggling several notions at once regarding his school's disappointing results on the national examinations, believing that no single reason can be pinpointed for anything that happens in a school. In his view, whenever principals want to improve student outcomes, they must take into account the whole spectrum of factors that may be affecting them. Later in the interview, John shared that he did not just sit back and criticize but made some attempts to help his teachers understand systemic principles too.

In line with this view, school leaders aiming to improve student achievements should monitor not only the achievements themselves but also various factors affecting them. Systems thinking facilitates the integration of a wide range of data, as illustrated by Gregory, with 14 years of experience as a high school principal. Gregory described how he derived meaning from his school's annual external evaluation exams, which measure three main factors: student achievement, pedagogical environment, and school climate:

- "The most important thing in this annual report, for me and for my superiors too, is student achievement. But, to understand why we got the results we did, I look for patterns in all of the data. I examine in which of the other areas the results are similar to students' scores on the achievement tests, and when I find similar patterns I understand the connections between climate, pedagogy, and outcomes."

Seeking to identify relationships among the information bits available to him, Gregory demonstrated systems thinking by distinguishing recurring patterns and linking various elements in school life together, in order to derive meaning from their combinations and treat the problem systemically. Identifying major patterns in testing data enables principals to look for the fundamental causes of test results rather than referring to symptoms, thus getting to the root of a problem by looking at the whole unruly bundle of roots underlying it.

Another important aspect of instructional leaders' interpretation of performance data involves temporal issues. When schools invest efforts into improving student achievement, they obviously expect to attain better future outcomes. From the systems thinking perspective, school principals must understand that oftentimes actions taken to promote students' achievements will not yield immediate results. Problems may arise when principals are not aware of the impact of this delay that is often inherent to the complex processes leading to improved achievement.

In some cases, lack of awareness about time delays may lead principals to give up on certain plans entirely. Barbara, with 11 years of experience as a junior high school principal, discussed the importance of such temporal awareness when describing how she was currently analyzing her school's assessment data. Although her school was in the midst of a large-scale change, and the results seemed quite disappointing, Barbara did not give up:

- "We need to carefully examine what we are not doing right. Our improvement efforts require a considerable investment of resources, time, and purposeful attention, and the results are indeed disappointing. However, I believe that the fruits of our efforts may become noticeable only after some time. We have to make decisions prudently, and we shouldn't shelve our improvement plan too early."

Barbara had taken the available data to heart. Nevertheless, she adjusted her decisions about next steps to account for her knowledge about the sometimes convoluted working of systems over time. She considered that there may be a case of delayed feedback here because of possible time lags occurring between the action taken and the appearance of its expected results. Thus, she was trying not to overreact, which could dampen the system's large-scale efforts. Instead, she maintained a systemic view that allowed for more optimism, predicting that multiple underlying effects might still yield the desired results later.

To summarize, research on principals' perceptions suggests that systems thinking may contribute to instructional leadership application by enabling school leaders to interpret and use available data wisely. This holistic perspective allows principals to take a wide variety of available factors into consideration, facilitating better data analysis and evidence-based decision making.

CONCLUSION

Systems thinking is not merely a *tool* for school leaders but rather is a school leadership approach, where the term "approach" refers to a comprehensive way of both conceptualizing and practicing within the entire work setting. Systems thinking may be seen as a worldview or perspective about school leadership, which offers a way to consider events, people, and processes.

Moreover, systems thinking may offer an effective way for principals to reference everyday school life, ongoing management issues, and numerous diverse aspects of their work. Thus, systems thinking can help school leaders cope with various kinds of administrative tasks, large and small, essential and marginal. It may be applied flexibly, as an efficient ongoing way to address short-term and long-term management issues across local and global aspects of organizational management.

Significantly, systems thinking may facilitate some of the core activities facing school leaders as they strive to improve teaching and learning in their school: creating a school curriculum in which the whole is greater than the sum of its parts, developing a school-based learning community to develop teachers' professionalism, and interpreting performance data effectively. Thus, systems thinking may be seen as one of the enablers of instructional leadership application.

PRACTICAL RECOMMENDATIONS ON SYSTEMS THINKING AS AN ENABLER OF INSTRUCTIONAL LEADERSHIP APPLICATION FOR POLICYMAKERS, PRINCIPAL EDUCATORS, SUPERINTENDENTS, AND PRINCIPALS

- Principals should align standards, curriculum, instruction, and evaluation, seeing the "forest," rather than just focusing on its parts, the "trees."
- Principals should improve their schools' curriculum holistically, both vertically (up and down the different age levels) and horizontally (across different disciplines).
- Principals should see their team as a collaborative group of individuals working together to achieve a common instructional goal, to allow the development of a professional learning community in the school.
- Principals should listen to the varied voices of staff, so that school leaders can be nurtured by the system too, and not just nurture their staff.
- Principals should always remember that every element within the large and complex school system as a whole inevitably has various reasons, explanations, and implications.
- Principals should understand that in many cases, actions taken to improve teaching and learning will not yield immediate results.

REFERENCES

Arnold, R. D., & Wade, J. P. (2015). A definition of systems thinking: A systems approach. *Procedia Computer Science, 44*, 669–678.

Brenninkmeyer, L. D., & Spillane, J. P. (2008). Problem-solving processes of expert and typical school principals: A quantitative look. *School Leadership and Management, 28*(5), 435–468.

Checkland, P. (1999). *Systems thinking, systems practice; Soft systems methodology: A 30 year retrospective.* Wiley.

Descartes, R. (1985). *The philosophical writings of Descartes* (J. Cottingham, R. Stoothof, & D. Murdoch, Trans.). Cambridge University Press.

DuFour, R., DuFour, R., Eaker, R., Mattos, M., & Muhammed, A. (2021). *Revisiting professional learning communities at work: Proven insights for sustained, substantive school improvement.* Solution Tree.

Richmond, B. (1994). System dynamics/systems thinking: Let's just get on with it. *System Dynamics Review, 10*(2–3), 135–157.

Robinson, V. M. J. (2010). From instructional leadership to leadership capabilities: Empirical findings and methodological challenges. *Leadership and Policy in Schools, 9*(1), 1–26.

Senge, P. (1990). *The fifth discipline: The art and practice of the learning organization.* Doubleday.

Senge, P. M. (2014). *The fifth discipline fieldbook: Strategies and tools for building a learning organization.* Currency.

Shaked, H., Benoliel, P., Nadav, N., & Schechter, C. (2018). Principals' systems thinking: The meaning and measure of a leadership construct. In H. Shaked, C. Schechter, & A. J. Daly (Eds.), *Leading holistically: How schools, districts, and states improve systemically* (pp. 54–73). Routledge.

Shaked, H., & Schechter, C. (2014). Systems school leadership: Exploring an emerging construct. *Journal of Educational Administration, 52*(6), 792–811.

Shaked, H., & Schechter, C. (2016). Holistic school leadership: Systems thinking as an instructional leadership enabler. *Bulletin of the National Association of Secondary School Principals, 100*(4), 177–202.

Shaked, H., & Schechter, C. (2017). *Systems thinking for school leaders: Holistic leadership for excellence in education.* Springer.

PART II

Inhibitors of Instructional Leadership Application

The present part of this book explores factors that may inhibit instructional leadership, which may account for why principals demonstrate instructional leadership only in part. Chapter 4 first reviews the obstacles of instructional leadership discussed in the existing research literature and then suggests a new type of obstacle—inhibitory perceptions of principals. Chapter 5 then concentrates on clan culture, which can inhibit certain instructional leadership functions. Chapter 6 raises the question of how the national context may interfere with the application of instructional leadership. For this purpose, it discusses low power distance, which refers to the extent to which a specific society expects and accepts that power is unequally distributed between individuals. Next, Chapter 7 investigates the application of instructional leadership in rural areas, because rural education is not functioning well enough in many countries around the globe.

Chapter 4

Perceptions Inhibiting Instructional Leadership Application

ABSTRACT

The current chapter extends previously available knowledge on the factors inhibiting instructional leadership application by illustrating how these inhibitory factors involve not only constraints on school principals and their capabilities but also school leaders' deep disagreements with the conceptual framework that underpins instructional leadership. Particularly, this chapter adds three main inhibitory perceptions to the literature: (1) perceptions regarding the role of the principal; (2) perceptions regarding the goal of schooling; and (3) perceptions regarding principal-teacher relationships. Practical recommendations related to the perceptions inhibiting the application of instructional leadership are offered at the end of the chapter.

FACTORS PREVIOUSLY IDENTIFIED AS INHIBITING INSTRUCTIONAL LEADERSHIP APPLICATION

Despite long-standing efforts by researchers, policymakers, and educators to campaign for instructional leadership's prioritization as possibly the most important component of the school principal's role, several studies have shown that the time devoted by principals to instructional leadership application is insufficient. Research over the past 35 years consistently demonstrates that principals spend minimal amounts of time on instructional leadership activities (Goldring et al., 2020).

Using observational time use data for all high school principals in one district in Miami, Horng and her colleagues (2010) found that principals appear to allocate a very limited percentage of their time to instruction-related activities such as day-to-day instruction tasks (6%) and more general instructional program responsibilities (7%). Similarly, May and Supovitz (2011), who examined principals' daily logs, reported that on average, principals spent only 8% of their time on instructional leadership activities. Investigating 100 urban principals across three school years, Grissom and his colleagues (2013) also found that only 13% of principals' time was directed to instructional leadership application.

In each of two other studies, only 19% of principals' time was devoted to providing instructional leadership in their schools (Camburn et al., 2010; May et al., 2012). Even at the end of the second decade of the 21st century, the situation is not much different because principals still spend minimal amounts of time on instructional leadership activities (Goldring et al., 2020).

Considering the substantial efforts that have been invested by diverse professionals to encourage and support principals' instructional leadership application, these statistics are extremely disappointing. In view of principals' continued limited involvement in applying instructional leadership, a significant question arises: Why do school principals not devote more time to instructional leadership application? In other words, why do they not give instructional leadership a central place in their principalship practices?

In answer to this question, three main barriers to instructional leadership application have been mentioned in the literature: minimal available time, inadequate pedagogical knowledge, and deeply implanted organizational norms (e.g., Cuban, 1988; Goldring et al., 2008, 2015, 2020; Prytula et al., 2013).

First, principals are said to lack sufficient time to engage directly in attempts to improve teaching and learning, largely because of ongoing structural limits on principals' time that pressure them to attend to other issues like buildings' operations or student affairs. Observers have noted that instructional leadership application often conflicts with the tasks involved in the day-to-day management of schools.

Moreover, while instructional leadership application requires uninterrupted blocks of time for activities such as planning, writing, conferencing, observing, analyzing curriculum, and developing professional growth activities for staff, the average workday of principals is characterized by fragmentation of activities and brevity of attention to issues. Inasmuch as considerable time is spent on unplanned and crisis-oriented issues, principals' efforts to work on instructional matters for the necessary prolonged blocks of time seldom reach fruition during day-to-day school operations. A case in point is discussed later (see Chapter 8) regarding principals' difficulties prioritizing uninterrupted time blocks for teacher evaluation.

A second inhibitory factor of instructional leadership application that was previously identified in the literature is principals' inadequate relevant knowledge base. Principals have often been described as lacking the explicit knowledge needed to function as instructional leaders (the types of knowledge that principals saw as enablers of instructional leadership application and the types of knowledge that were viewed as unnecessary were discussed above in Chapter 1).

Third, deep-seated organizational norms that are prevalent in many schools can push principals away from instructional leadership application. In particular, school stakeholders may traditionally view instruction as the singular domain of teachers alone rather than as a domain appropriate for principals' direct involvement (Goldring et al., 2015). These norms have been described as deterring principals from "encroaching" on the territory of teachers, who may be reluctant to relinquish their unique position in the in-school hierarchy. Such prescriptive norms expecting principals to "stay in their managerial lane" were described by Murphy and colleagues (2016, p. 462):

> When school leaders "left teaching," they immediately set themselves up as something different from teachers and an occupation different from teaching. They were no longer teachers. They did not want to be teachers. They were not in the teaching business. . . . They were managers and administrators.

Inasmuch as principals cannot physically enter each classroom, they must rely on teachers to make desired instructional changes and therefore must contend with the professional norms prevailing in the school. When those norms decree that the classroom is the exclusive domain of teachers, principals who wish to lead learning will receive limited formal authority from their teachers to act. In such cases, principals often informally trade their authority over curriculum and instruction for compliance by teachers on other issues (see also Chapter 6 regarding the power of national norms).

Overall, prior literature has indicated that researchers believe in school leaders' intentions and willingness to become instructional leaders: "Most principals have a strong intention . . . to engage in the tasks of instructional leadership" (Hallinger & Murphy, 2013, p. 10). Unfortunately, these intentions are often not realized because of pressures exerted on school principals (e.g., time constraints, norms) and due to their insufficient capabilities (e.g., knowledge gaps). Thus, the literature has identified a powerful set of forces drawing even well-intentioned principals away from engagement in instructional leadership application.

Now, in addition to these inhibitory forces, recent research findings can further extend available knowledge on other factors that may reduce principals' actual implementation of instructional leadership. Specifically, principals' own inhibitory perceptions—the ways in which principals look at, understand, and interpret the instructional leadership approach—may hold important implications for their behavior.

Namely, my recent study (Shaked, 2019) highlighted principals' deep disagreements with the conceptual framework that underpins instructional leadership. Specifically, this study has identified three main perception-related factors that may inhibit principals' application of instructional leadership in their schools: (1) perceptions regarding the role of the principal; (2) perceptions regarding the goal of schooling; and (3) perceptions regarding principal-teacher relationships.

Perceptions of School Leaders' Roles as Inhibitors of Instructional Leadership

The first perception found in my study (Shaked, 2019) as inhibiting instructional leadership application concerned many principals' views about their role definition. While the instructional leadership approach expects principals to be significantly involved in the development of curriculum and instruction in order to improve pupils' performance, some principals disagreed with that focus—believing that they should be concentrating mainly on other areas.

Instead of focusing on teaching and learning, several principals placed major emphasis on their central role as a bridge to the extra-school world, which includes—among others—the district, the school board, and the parents' committee. For example, Dawn, with four years of experience as a high school principal, explained: "While the entire staff is taking care of what is going on inside the school, I am the only contact person with all the outside parties. Therefore, this is a main component of my job." In addition, some principals underscored the principal's vital role as manager of the school's resources and budget as demanding substantial time from them throughout the school year, thereby competing with instructional leadership applications.

More broadly, some principals perceived their leadership role as one of simply enabling teachers to do their jobs rather than "interfering" with teachers' work, thus rejecting the primary philosophy underlying instructional leadership. Expressing the attitude that instruction can be well handled by the school's teachers and mid-level leaders without principals' direct involvement, such leaders expressed the belief that their main role is to give teachers the means to carry out their work and to establish the conditions that would allow teachers to succeed.

In this vein, Juanita, with 17 years of experience as an elementary school principal, said that her main task is to "facilitate." She explained: "To do a good job, teachers need proper conditions. When I take care of all the necessary resources and create an atmosphere of discipline in the school, teachers can do the good work they know how to do." Thus, Juanita placed emphasis on aspects of her role other than that of instructional leader.

Other principals even considered their involvement in teaching and learning to be ineffectual for improving actual instruction in the school. Some even felt pessimistic about their involvement making any meaningful impact because of the intransigence of teachers' ineffective or problematic behaviors. As described by Christine, with seven years of experience as an elementary school principal: "People do not change."

Overall, these principals' perceptions about their desired or feasible roles served to constrain their attempts to act as instructional leaders. Instead, they focused mainly on aspects of the principal role related to setting up the proper conditions for teachers in terms of logistic arrangements, ensuring adequate budgets, and dealing with student discipline, as well as adapting organizational activities in order to conform to the expectations of external stakeholders. Therefore, they simply did not accept the main claim espoused by the instructional leadership approach—whereby principals are expected to engage primarily, first and foremost, in activities that are clearly designed to improve teaching and learning.

Perceptions of the Goal of Schooling as Inhibitors of Instructional Leadership Application

The second perception found in my study (Shaked, 2019) as inhibiting instructional leadership application concerned principals' perceptions about the goal of schooling. Some principals claimed that they should simply not be dedicating too much of their focus to improving teaching and learning because ensuring students' academic success is not the most important thing that a school should do. For some principals, the school's primary task should be a non-academic, socializing one, that is, to meet students' emotional needs, support their social integration, and impart moral values.

These principals ascribed primary importance to the school's role in developing students' emotional well-being, including their sense of belonging and safety, happiness in the present, and optimism regarding the future. Moreover, these principals often distinguished between "instruction" and "education," claiming that schools are indeed required to teach their students through academic instruction, but that their first and foremost goal should be to edify students by developing them morally and promoting their humanistic and adaptive character traits such as responsibility, self-control, integrity, decency, and good manners.

Roger, with 21 years of experience as a high school teacher, clarified this view: "Yes, schools should teach students literacy, math, foreign languages, and science, but above all and before anything else, we must foster personal responsibility and arouse a sense of mission." Similarly, Jean, with six years of experience as a high school principal, asserted: "Prioritizing students' academic progress is based on a narrow point of view, which considers schools as only preparing students for college and the workforce. Raising young people of values is no less important."

Teresa, with seven years of experience as an elementary school principal, distinctly disagreed with the emphasis given to grades and achievements: "It is shortsighted to define a school's success based on student achievements alone. Test scores are not all that matters."

In particular, principals who emphasized school's main task as a non-academic one noted that a school is a mini-community that reflects the larger, more mature society. Therefore, they upheld that schools should give their students the social tools required to function within their society.

For example, such tools may include teaching students to navigate social interactions with peers from different backgrounds and helping them become productive community members who work not only toward their own interests but also on behalf of public interests. Importantly, these principals wanted their students to learn to be tolerant and accept people who differed from them.

Several principals maintained that they should devote time to ensuring that their schools develop students' identity. Victor, with three years of experience as a high school principal, concentrated on his students' religious identity: "For me, developing our students' religious identity is the most important thing we do here, because religious identity provides them a perspective from which to view everything, including academic studies."

Wendy, with seven years of experience as a junior high school principal, said: "High achievements are essential, but they are foundations only. Above them, we have to build the really important thing, which is the personality of the student."

More broadly, principals who espoused a non-academic chief aim for their school claimed that schools play a significant role in preparing students to become future citizens of the world, accentuating the importance of the school in promoting students' future participation in the democratic process, in instilling loyalty to their homeland, and in increasing awareness concerning social justice. Jack, with six years of experience as an elementary school principal, explained his rationale for upholding this socializing view:

- "Learning is very important, but it should be seen as a means to an end. We spend so much time measuring what our students know that we have so little time left to focus on who they are. We should not be surprised, then, if they become people we don't like or respect, or if we end up worrying about their future contribution to society."

Perceptions of Principal-Teacher Relationships as Inhibitors of Instructional Leadership Application

The third inhibitory perception found in my study (Shaked, 2019) concerned principals' belief that by applying an instructional leadership approach, they could damage their principal-teacher relationships. Interestingly, this finding seems to contradict principals' aforementioned emphasis on healthy relationships with teachers as a crucial enabler of instructional leadership application (as discussed above in Chapter 2).

According to this inhibitory perspective voiced by a number of principals, although positive principal-teacher relationships are considered to be of utmost significance in order to engage with teachers in productive and respectful conversations about the quality of teaching and learning, such relationships may be undermined if principals must continually review their teachers' practice in keeping with an instructional leadership role.

Beatrice, with seven years of experience as an elementary school principal, explained how instructional supervision may impinge on relationships with teachers: "Principals should pay attention not only to the educational work that needs to be carried out, but also to their relations with the teaching staff. You can't simultaneously supervise the teachers and nurture your relationship with them." In Beatrice's eyes, the instructional leader's role as a continuous evaluator of her teachers' instruction quality contradicted her ability to sustain the good relationships that she needed with those teachers in order to enhance the school's productivity. This inherent contradiction is discussed further in Chapter 8.

Indeed, the interviewed principals in my study claimed that smoothly running a school requires both abilities—not only the ability to accomplish the goal of increasing student outcomes but also the ability to foster positive relationships with teachers in order to achieve their cooperation and infuse a pleasant atmosphere. Therefore, they argued that controlling the teachers' work too closely is not recommended.

This perspective somewhat echoes the transformational leadership approach, which focuses on building trust, supporting the needs of teachers, and making school goals personal goals of teachers. Norma, with five years of experience as an elementary school principal, articulated her dilemma clearly:

- "To produce school graduates with the highest possible achievements, we necessarily have processes designed to monitor teaching quality . . . [however,] good principal-teacher relationships are [also] important for student achievement, and these two things are not really compatible, because close monitoring inevitably spoils relationships."

Rachel, with two years of experience as a high school principal, asserted that principals should limit instructional leadership application even if that causes a certain decrease in academic results: "Even if it lowers our achievements a bit, I believe a principal should be patient and considerate. You work with people here; it's not a machine."

In short, while principals indeed ascribed importance to improving teaching and learning, they also feared that activities aimed at achieving this goal might negatively affect their relationships with teachers, which they considered to be essential for a well-functioning school without the resentments and revolts of teachers. Moreover, many similar comments by principals highlighted perceptions of in-school relationships not only as necessary but also as resembling those in a family, which elicited loyalty conflicts between principals' work pressures and closeness to longtime friends who feel like family.

Therefore, all in all, principals' perceptions about their work relationships were a clear inhibitory factor, resulting in their only partial or limited enactment of instructional leadership activities. For more on this issue, see the following chapter on the challenges inherent to clan-type culture.

CONCLUSION

Extending beyond prior research that attempted to explain why principals tend to regard instructional leadership as holding only secondary importance, my study (Shaked, 2019) highlighted several deep-rooted perceptions held by principals that might play a part in principals' frequent avoidance of this leadership approach. Slightly differing from inhibitory factors yielded by prior research, the inhibitory factors of instructional leadership application found in my study do not only involve the constraints on and capabilities of school principals.

To a large extent, the perceptions uncovered by these interviewed principals reflect their deep disagreements with the conceptual framework underlying instructional leadership. Principals were preoccupied with the potential damage that instructional leadership might cause to their good relations with teachers, which, paradoxically, could reduce teachers' willingness to become invested in improving teaching and learning.

In addition, principals did not see eye to eye with instructional leadership's recommended academic focus for their job because they often placed high value on the non-academic, humanistic, ethical, and social goals of schooling. They also did not necessarily agree with the priorities and principles set by instructional leadership precepts, instead viewing any direct principal involvement in teaching to be more akin to interference. Hence, principals often chose to emphasize many leadership functions other than the instructional one.

PRACTICAL RECOMMENDATIONS REGARDING INHIBITORY PERCEPTIONS OF INSTRUCTIONAL LEADERSHIP APPLICATION FOR POLICYMAKERS, PRINCIPAL EDUCATORS, SUPERINTENDENTS, AND PRINCIPALS

- Principals should recognize the need to find a balance between healthy principal-teacher relationships conducive to instructional leadership application and the desire to prevent tensions in the relationships, which might serve to inhibit such leadership activities.
- Principals should understand that they have to cultivate "good enough"—rather than overly good and positive—relationships with their teachers, with a focus on mutual respect and shared goals.
- Principals should be provided with opportunities to learn how to monitor teaching quality and student achievement alongside simultaneous cultivation of positive principal-teacher relationships by using respectful growth-supportive communication and constructively critical feedback.
- Principals should continually receive convincing theoretical rationales and new research-based information supporting the significance of their role as instructional leaders, on an ongoing basis, without assuming that principals have internalized this leadership style.
- Principal educators and supervisors should give school leaders opportunities to discuss instructional leadership's premises in a safe space where they can openly disclose their concerns, disagreements, and resistance to fundamental instructional leadership tenets such as the need for principals to focus on learning and academic success as the ultimate goal of schooling.
- The paradoxical approach as enabling instructional leadership application despite inhibitory perceptions is discussed below in Chapter 11.

REFERENCES

Camburn, E., Spillane, J., & Sebastian, J. (2010). Assessing the utility of a daily log for measuring principal leadership practice. *Educational Administration Quarterly, 46*(5), 707–737.

Cuban, L. (1988). *Managerial imperative and the practice of leadership in schools.* SUNY Press.

Goldring, E., Grissom, J. A., Neumerski, C. M., Blissett, R., Murphy, J., & Porter, A. (2020). Increasing principals' time on instructional leadership: Exploring the SAM® process. *Journal of Educational Administration, 58*(1), 19–37.

Goldring, E., Grissom, J. A., Neumerski, C. M., Murphy, J., Blissett, R., & Porter, A. (2015). *Making time for instructional leadership.* http://www.wallacefoundation.org/knowledge-center/Pages/Making-Time-for-Instructional-Leadership.aspx

Goldring, E., Huff, J., May, H., & Camburn, E. (2008). School context and individual characteristics: What influences principal practice? *Journal of Educational Administration, 46*(3), 332–352.

Grissom, J. A., Loeb, S., & Master, B. (2013). Effective instructional time use for school leaders: Longitudinal evidence from observations of principals. *Educational Researcher, 42*(8), 433–444.

Hallinger, P., & Murphy, J. F. (2013). Running on empty? Finding the time and capacity to lead learning. *Bulletin of the National Association of Secondary School Principals, 97*(1), 5–21.

Horng, E. L., Klasik, D., & Loeb, S. (2010). Principal's time use and school effectiveness. *American Journal of Education, 116*(4), 491–523.

May, H., Huff, J., & Goldring, E. (2012). A longitudinal study of principals' activities and student performance. *School Effectiveness and School Improvement, 23*(4), 417–439.

May, H., & Supovitz, J. A. (2011). The scope of principal efforts to improve instruction. *Educational Administration Quarterly, 47*(2), 332–352.

Murphy, J., Neumerski, C. M., Goldring, E., Grissom, J., & Porter, A. (2016). Bottling fog? The quest for instructional management. *Cambridge Journal of Education, 46*(4), 455–471.

Prytula, M., Noonan, B., & Hellsten, L. (2013). Toward instructional leadership: Principals perceptions of large-scale assessment in schools. *Canadian Journal of Educational Administration and Policy, 140,* 1–30.

Shaked, H. (2019). Perceptual inhibitors of instructional leadership in Israeli principals. *School Leadership & Management, 39*(5), 519–536.

Chapter 5

Clan Culture as an Inhibitor of Instructional Leadership Application

ABSTRACT

The previous chapter (and others) showed how a strong desire to establish close principal-teacher relationships might serve as an inhibitor of instructional leadership application. The present chapter goes on to elaborate how clan culture, which is a family-like work environment with strong bonds of loyalty and tight interpersonal relationships, inhibits instructional leadership application. It points to three functions of instructional leadership that may be weakened when principals are influenced by this organizational culture: supervising and evaluating instruction, protecting instructional time, and providing incentives for teachers. The chapter closes by offering practical recommendations about the application of instructional leadership under clan culture.

WHAT IS CLAN CULTURE?

The previous chapter argued that overemphasized principal-teacher relationships can inhibit instructional leadership application (see Chapter 4). In fact, the difficulty to reconcile interpersonal relationships with instructional leadership application is one of the main topics addressed in this book.

To deepen exploration of this potential conflict, my recent study (Shaked, in press) sought to understand how a school's "clan culture" work environment may inhibit its principal's application of instructional leadership. The family-like clan culture is characterized by strong bonds of loyalty and tight interpersonal relationships in the organization.

Clan culture is one of the four types of culture depicted by Cameron and Quinn (2011) in their organizational culture typology, which is based on a dual-axis model. The vertical axis examines whether an organization is focused more on stability or on flexibility. The horizontal axis examines whether the organization looks more outward or inward.

The way organizations prioritize these competing values determines the types of cultures that emerge within them. Thus, the model is called a "competing values framework." The two axes of the model create four types of cultures: market (stability/outward), hierarchy (stability/inward), adhocracy (flexibility/outward), and clan (flexibility/inward).

Under a market culture, organizations are very aware of their position in the market and are determined to improve it. Such competitive organizations are results-based workplaces that are built on the dynamics of competition. Therefore, they emphasize meeting targets and deadlines.

Under a hierarchy culture, organizations prefer control and a structured working environment, in which procedures determine what the people do. Maintaining a smooth-running organization is of utmost importance. Formal rules and policy documents hold the organization together, and the values include consistency and uniformity.

Under an adhocracy culture, organizations prefer innovation and risk taking in order to meet external expectations as quickly as possible. These organizations are held together by their desire to develop quickly. Therefore, they are dynamic and entrepreneurial, constantly creating new products and finding innovative ways to succeed.

Under a clan culture, the members of the organization share commonalities and see themselves as part of one big, cohesive family. A sense of "we-ness" is the "glue" that holds clan-type organizations together, and their theory of effectiveness is based on human empowerment and participation. In clan cultures, leaders are seen as mentors and team builders and perhaps even as parent figures. All employees are equal, taking part in decision-making processes. Teamwork, collaboration, and consensus are of paramount importance.

Insofar as the clan culture is focused on flexibility rather than stability (the vertical axis of Cameron and Quinn's model), rules and regulations are of secondary importance. Leaving room for discretion is more important than adherence to procedures, and a positive climate and concern for people are more important than control and supervision. At the same time, the clan culture looks inward more than outward (the horizontal axis of Cameron and Quinn's model); hence, the work atmosphere is pleasant for employees, but there is not always a commitment to providing optimal service to customers.

Critics of clan culture assert that it can reduce effectiveness if employees use it as an opportunity to spend time doing nothing rather than contributing to shared goals. Similarly, freedom and autonomy may be used as an excuse to do nothing useful or even to deal with private matters at the expense of working time. It may also be problematic when team members disagree on an important issue. Without a strong authority figure, good ideas that can advance the organization may be abandoned simply because they do not get a majority vote.

The clan culture is intensified in schools as a result of the longevity of principal-teacher relationships. In many cases, teachers work for many, many years in the same school, and principals often hold the job for years too. Some of the principals were previously teachers at the same school. Even a new principal coming into a school where the teachers have all been working side by side for many years could face pressures to conform to the school's existing clan culture norms.

My study (Shaked, in press) found that schools leaning more toward a clan culture had a negative impact on principals' instructional leadership application. Specifically, this recent research identified three functions necessary for effective instructional leadership that were weakened when principals were influenced by a clan culture in their school: supervising and evaluating instruction, protecting instructional time, and providing incentives for teachers.

Supervising and Evaluating Instruction in Clan Culture

The first function of instructional leadership that was found to be hindered by clan culture was principals' supervision and evaluation of instruction in the school. This function of instructional leadership entails supporting teachers in putting the school's instructional goals into practice, developing teachers' thinking about their instructional decisions, directing them to notice and address weak areas in their teaching, helping them improve, monitoring the extent of curricular implementation, and so forth.

While classroom observations are a valuable means of supervising the quality of teaching, principals who were influenced by clan culture rarely observed classes so that they would not have to criticize the teachers' practice. When they were required to use impressions from classroom observations to evaluate teachers who were candidates for tenure or promotion to higher ranks, they did not utilize this process to improve teaching quality, but rather they gave higher ratings than what they thought these teachers deserved (see Chapter 8).

Amanda, with 10 years of experience as an elementary school principal, explicitly compared her school to a warm family unit: "Our school is like one big family." From her perspective, the familial ambience did not allow for tough teacher evaluation: "If I were to perform teacher evaluations like I was asked to do, it might heavily change our family-like atmosphere."

In such a clan culture, low performance on national achievement tests was not seen by principals as a sufficient reason to criticize teachers. Albert, with 11 years of experience as an elementary school principal, asserted: "Failure of an entire class indicates a problem but does not always mean that the teacher is not good enough. Some students have difficulty passing exams, while others do not have enough motivation." He concluded: "Criticism of teachers for student failure is not the right way to improve their work."

Doris, with four years of experience as a junior high school principal, claimed that the perception of teachers as responsible for students' outcomes has negative consequences: "Blaming teachers for students' poor performance does not lead to further effort by teachers or to improving their teaching methods. It leads to cheating, narrowing the curriculum to emphasize test content, and teaching directly for the test."

Even when it came to teachers who were consistently ineffective, principals who saw them as part of the family took an inclusive approach and did not push for dismissal, to avoid economic harm to their "family member." Thus, in line with the inward/flexible axes of the clan culture typology (Cameron & Quinn, 2011), to maintain a pleasant work climate and avoid threatening employees' sense of we-ness, principals appear to compromise on their commitment to providing optimal services to their students.

This inhibiting effect of clan culture specifically on principals' supervision and evaluation of instruction in schools has broad implications because the research is clear: Students' academic performance depends crucially on the effectiveness of their teachers. Teaching quality is the most significant school-related factor influencing student achievement (Darling-Hammond, 2000; Stronge et al., 2007). Therefore, by retaining poorly performing teachers, principals agreed to lower the quality of teaching in their school (see Chapter 9).

Protecting Instructional Time in Clan Culture

The second function of instructional leadership that was found to be impaired by clan culture was principals' protection of time devoted to teaching and learning. This function focuses on the actions taken by the principal to ensure that the precious resource of instructional time is not lost.

To this end, effective instructional leaders are those who ensure that teachers are punctual, do not schedule other school activities during class time, employ classroom management strategies that allow maximum utilization of available teaching time, and the like. Principals who safeguard instructional time in their schools also establish a sufficient mechanism for ensuring that absent teachers provide substitute teachers with meaningful assignments for their students.

In contrast, under clan culture, principals often saw teacher absenteeism as an acceptable phenomenon and an inherent part of school life, and they made only limited efforts to reduce its scope. Expressing family-like loyalty to their staff, the interviewed principals claimed that their teachers made every possible attempt to attend class: "When a teacher does not come to school, I have no reason to put pressure on her, because I'm sure she has a good reason for it" (Raymond, with five years of experience as a junior high school principal).

Thus, principals in a clan culture did not raise any difficulties for teachers who wanted to be absent. Taking off two weeks to help take care of a new grandchild or a week before the teacher's daughter's wedding were considered reasonable, which could indicate over-identification of principals with teachers' family-work conflict.

When influenced by clan culture, principals also showed leniency when teachers were late for school or late for class after recess. For these principals, arriving on time was not more important than any of the many other qualities of a good teacher: "One of my teachers is consistently late. It is not uncommon for him to appear 15, 20, and even 30 minutes late. But he also has many merits. So why should I just look at his lateness?" (Henry, with 13 years of experience as a high school principal).

Principals did not describe any consequences for chronic tardiness or absenteeism. Similarly, many clan-motivated principals did not protect the time set aside for teachers' professional learning meetings, meetings to discuss student grades or school policies, and parent meetings, turning a blind eye to teachers' late arrival and even to the absence of teachers from such activities.

In order to avoid burdening teachers, principals who acted in accordance with clan culture allowed teachers to attend meetings with parents or other teachers at the expense of lessons they were meant to teach. When a solution had to be found for the class while the teacher was attending such a meeting, these clan-driven principals only prioritized wanting to keep the students quiet and safe, without taking the loss of teaching and learning time into account.

Moreover, principals influenced by clan culture did not make sure that the teachers used their own instructional time properly. They did not require them to plan their lessons in advance so that the students would be able to learn more and would become more actively engaged during the instructional time. In addition, in the final weeks of the school year, they allowed teachers to screen films instead of exploiting precious class time for teaching.

Providing Incentives for Teachers in Clan Culture

The third function of instructional leadership that was found to be impeded by clan culture was principals' provision of incentives for teachers. This function pertains to the quality and consistency of the recognition and appreciation that a principal gives teachers for their teaching quality and their students' successes.

When clan culture had an influence on principals, they believed that giving incentives for teachers might arouse envy among their colleagues, much like when parents are seen as choosing favorites, thereby undermining the school's warm family atmosphere. Carrie, with seven years of experience as an elementary school principal, considered the idea of awarding prizes to teachers who had the fewest absences during the school year. However, the senior management team in her school recommended that she not do so, suggesting to her that "placing one teacher at the top may make other people resentful, so while making one teacher happy, you make others miserable."

Similarly, with two years of experience as a high school principal, Billy said: "Each year one of the teachers wins a free vacation, in appreciation of their educational work. I am against this initiative because it only provokes controversy among the teaching staff."

The principals who were influenced by clan culture not only failed to give incentives for teachers whose practices were above the expected standard, but they were also forgiving or lenient, rather than strict or tough, when teachers' practices were below or contrary to the standards expected.

For example, such principals did not respond harshly to non-compliance with deadlines. Although delays diminish the effectiveness of teaching work, these principals overlooked teachers' failure to submit annual planning documents, student achievement mapping, or report card grades by the set date. They accepted late submissions as normative behavior: "I take into account in advance that teachers will not submit grades on time, so I set an early deadline" (Rhonda, with 19 years of experience as an elementary school principal).

They were pessimistic about their effectiveness in dealing with such teacher behavior: "Some teachers meet deadlines, but others do not. There's nothing one can do" (Bernice, with 11 years of experience as an elementary school principal). Or as Samantha, with nine years of experience as an elementary school principal, complained: "I remind them over and over again to submit the mappings, but there are some who will not submit at all."

Providing incentives for teachers expresses prioritization for quality teaching, which directly affects student learning and results. In contrast, under clan culture, principals gave primary importance to the maintenance of positive relationships with and among the teaching staff.

Thus, instead of celebrating academic achievements, they arranged events that were designed to strengthen the cohesion within their team. Birthdays and other social gatherings were prominent features in their schools. Interviews with principals suggested that teachers internalized this message and therefore saw interpersonal relationships, rather than educational work, as their primary purpose when they came to the school.

Principals complained that teachers came mainly to meet their close friends on the teaching staff, and not necessarily their students. Principals asserted that teachers' most enjoyable time at school was the time they spent with their colleagues. They shared the impression that leaving the teachers' break room to enter the classroom was a moment that teachers tried to postpone for as long as possible.

CONCLUSION

Clan culture is an amicable working environment, in which people have a lot in common with each other and which to no small degree resembles an extended family. Based on the claim raised in the previous chapter that intense desire to create warm principal-teacher relationships may become an inhibitory perception of instructional leadership application (see Chapter 4 and Shaked, 2019), the current chapter sought to understand how the wider school climate's clan culture may influence principals' application of an instructional leadership approach.

Three functions of instructional leadership were found to be weakened when principals were influenced by clan culture. First, the strong respect for teacher autonomy and hesitation to express criticism associated with clan culture was found to inhibit principals' application of the instructional leadership function of *supervising and evaluating instruction*. Second, clan culture's family-like norms inhibited principals from applying the instructional leadership function of *protecting instructional time*; instead, principals avoided establishing unambiguous requirements to safeguard learning and teaching during class time. Third, the clan culture's norm of treating everyone kindly without favoritism inhibited principals' application of the instructional leadership function of *providing teachers with incentives*.

PRACTICAL RECOMMENDATIONS ON CLAN CULTURE FOR POLICYMAKERS, PRINCIPAL EDUCATORS, SUPERINTENDENTS, AND PRINCIPALS

- Principals should know that all organizational cultures promote some forms of behavior and inhibit others. Clan culture may inhibit the effective application of instructional leadership.
- Principals as instructional leaders should emphasize clear goals, supervision, and bottom-line results rather than teacher individualism and flexibility.
- Principals should protect instructional time by delegitimizing unjustified absences and tardiness. In taking these steps, principals can be supported by their superintendents, who can confirm that absences and tardiness are unacceptable.
- Principals should direct teachers to utilize lesson time properly toward instructional objectives and not allow competing activities to take place at the expense of lessons.
- Principals should establish an efficient mechanism to make sure that absent teachers provide substitute teachers with meaningful tasks for their students.
- Principals should treat all teachers equally but not in a way that is accepting of poor-quality teaching.

REFERENCES

Cameron, K. S., & Quinn, R. E. (2011). *Diagnosing and changing organisational culture: Based on the competing values framework*. Wiley.

Darling-Hammond, L. (2000). Teacher quality and student achievement. *Education Policy Analysis Archives, 8*(1), 1–44.

Shaked, H. (2019). Perceptual inhibitors of instructional leadership in Israeli principals. *School Leadership & Management, 39*(5), 519–536.

Shaked, H. (in press). How clan culture impairs functions of instructional leadership: The case of Israel. *Leadership and Policy in Schools*.

Stronge, J. H., Ward, T. J., Tucker, P. D., & Hindman, J. L. (2007). What is the relationship between teacher quality and student achievement? An exploratory study. *Journal of Personnel Evaluation In Education, 20*(3), 165–184.

Chapter 6

Low Power Distance as an Inhibitor of Instructional Leadership Application

ABSTRACT

This chapter raises the question of how schools' larger national context may inhibit instructional leadership application. As a case in point, research shows that low power distance as a sociocultural norm inhibits principals' adoption of instructional leadership in their role set. This case illustrates how despite increasing global acceptance of the instructional leadership approach, its application is inevitably shaped by the institutional policies and cultural values of different societies. Even when a "generic" model of leadership is adopted by policymakers, there will be a process of mutual adaptation during implementation. The chapter ends with workable recommendations about the application of instructional leadership under low power distance.

THE IMPACT OF NATIONAL CONTEXT

School leadership is influenced by the broader national context in many ways. For one, national context shapes institutional aspects such as principals' official job definitions and responsibilities through laws, policies, and qualification requirements. Another avenue of influence is via the sociocultural aspect of the national context, which shapes principals' behavior through a complex network of values and perceptions internalized through training and socialization processes. Both superiors and subordinates unconsciously judge the effectiveness of a principal's leadership according to the degree to which observable practices conform to national expectations and socioculturally accepted norms for desirable role behavior by the school's leader.

Because school leadership is context dependent, its conceptual frameworks are often interpreted and applied differently in various countries. One example of such cross-cultural differences involves the conceptual models of school leadership roles such as the instructional and transformational approaches that were developed in the United States. (Transformational leadership emphasizes building trust, supporting the needs of teachers, and transferring the school's goals to become staff's personal goals.) Examination of a sample of Norwegian principals showed that these two taxonomies for instructional and transformational leadership could not be replicated, implying different conceptualizations of school leadership in Nordic countries in comparison to the United States (Aas & Brandmo, 2016).

A second example of such cross-cultural differences concerns the leadership-for-learning framework, which integrates several earlier conceptualizations of school leadership (see Introduction). A recent study that analyzed an international survey identified three types of schools in the context of the "leadership for learning" framework worldwide—in contrast to only two school types in the United States. This research finding casts doubt on the effectiveness of narrowly applying U.S.-based research on leadership for learning around the globe for uses in policy, training, and practice, without attending to sociocultural and national influences (Bowers, 2020).

Although these two studies, as well as others, have shown that educational leadership is molded by the national context, the research literature on educational leadership often ignores or minimizes contextual influences (Clarke & O'Donoghue, 2017). The effects of the national context have been insufficiently explored regarding school leadership in general and instructional leadership in particular (Hallinger, 2018). Although the instructional leadership approach as a central feature of school principals' role is currently being investigated and implemented in many countries worldwide, we still do not know enough about how the application of instructional leadership is altered and shaped by the values, beliefs, and norms that comprise different societies.

Moreover, although instructional leadership has occupied a central place in educational discourse in the United States for over half a century, it has only spread noticeably to other parts of the world since the beginning of the 21st century. Given this reality, instructional leadership serves as a good example of policy (or practice) "borrowing." This refers to an intentional effort to improve an educational system through the introduction of a policy that originated in another national context (Nir et al., 2018).

Policy borrowing diminishes the need to "reinvent the wheel" when confronting similar challenges, reduces uncertainties associated with implementation, and offers previously tested justifications that may reduce resistance to change. However, policy borrowing can also introduce unanticipated problems that arise from differences between the originating and receiving societies regarding their sociocultural values and institutional policy frameworks.

Both positive and negative responses to "borrowed" policy models have been documented in the recent literature on instructional leadership (Ng et al., 2015; Pan et al., 2017; Qian et al., 2017; Steiner-Khamsi, 2016). As a case illustration, this chapter next presents research on a national context characterized by low power distance.

Instructional Leadership Application in a Low Power Distance Culture

The findings of our recent study (Shaked et al., 2020) reinforced theoretical assertions that national context influences the practices of school leaders not only through institutional rules, regulations, and job descriptions, but also through values, shared beliefs, and social norms. We found that Israeli principals were not applying instructional leadership in a manner that was consistent with prescriptions embedded in their policy frameworks and training curricula.

According to our interviewed principals, one significant force shaping instructional leadership application is low power distance. Power distance refers to the extent to which a society expects and accepts that power is distributed unevenly among people. Individuals in countries with "low power distance" such as Israel, Austria, New Zealand, or Denmark, tend to assume that all people are created equal, which may lead to behaviors indicating that people of lower rank in an organization hold little deference toward supposed authority figures.

In organizations with low power distance, those lower in the hierarchy may frequently interrupt authority figures' talk and may even question the decisions of those higher in the hierarchy, without any repercussions. In contrast, individuals in high power distance societies such as Malaysia, Panama, or Guatemala tend to rely on status differentiation and hierarchy to define social and work relationships (Hofstede, 2001).

In low power distance countries, respect is something that one earns by demonstrating hands-on expertise rather than by rank, age, social class, or gender. In the workplace, power is decentralized and shared, with managers relying on the experience and expertise of their subordinates. Employees expect consultation from their superiors and feel free to question them directly and openly.

Thus, workplaces tend to have a very informal atmosphere with direct communication among individuals, who operate on a first name basis. Less emphasis is placed on politeness and decorum, with intimate physical interpersonal space and loud conversation seen as more acceptable even in the workplace.

Our recent study (Shaked et al., 2020) revealed numerous ways in which low power distance norms appear to shape principals' application of instructional leadership in their schools. As mentioned above (Chapter 4), organizational norms are one of the inhibitory factors of instructional leadership application that were identified in previous research. Such norms push principals away from instructional leadership by setting unwritten boundaries regarding the extent to which principals can or cannot apply instructional leadership as a "top-down" leadership approach. Indeed, in our own study, we found that the national cultural norms for low power distance, which minimize workplace hierarchy and inequality, influenced principals' application of all four identified key elements of instructional leadership (as presented in the Introduction and Table 1): instructional vision, instructional program, instructional climate, and developing teachers.

Namely, with regard to instructional vision, the low power distance between school principals and their staff appeared to impact this first key element of instructional leadership, described by Hallinger and Murphy (1985). Specifically, low power distance seemed to influence the major dimension of *Defining the School Mission* (see Table 1), in terms of how that mission was developed.

Thus, our interviewed principals ascribed singular importance to the "collaborative" development of the school's mission. They believed that it was untenable for senior management to dictate the school's instructional goals. Instead, they assumed that the school's goals should be defined through a collaborative process that involves other stakeholders, especially teachers. As Brandon, with 18 years of experience as an elementary school principal, explained: "An inspiring and compelling vision is worth nothing if I created it alone."

The low power distance, however, had three challenging consequences for defining the school mission. First, the process of setting the school's goals often took longer than the principals would have liked: "Reaching an agreed vision takes longer than I thought" (Darlene, with five years of leadership experience as an elementary school principal). Second, the results were not always exactly what the principal might have wanted: "I can't force my vision on them. I have to compromise" (Shawn, with two years of experience as a high school principal). Third, with important ramifications for the principal's application of instructional leadership, the resulting mission and goals did not necessarily prioritize student learning outcomes as the school's main mission: "My teachers attach great importance to imparting values" (Nathan, with five years of experience as a junior high school principal).

Moreover, consistent with the tenets of a low power distance culture, principals did not expect their teachers to fully comply with the school's instructional mission, once it was defined. Instead, school leaders left room for teachers who disagreed with the mission to pursue somewhat differently weighted goals and approaches: "In the end, I can't really force my opinion on teachers" (Veronica, with 15 years of experience as an elementary school principal).

The impact of this low power distance culture on instructional leadership application was even stronger with respect to the second key element of instructional leadership, described by Hallinger and Murphy (1985) as the major dimension of *Managing the Instructional Program* (see Table 1). Some scholars have characterized instructional leadership as a "top-down school leadership model" due to functions embedded in this program management dimension, such as supervision and teacher evaluation (e.g., Aas & Brandmo, 2016).

Principals in low power distance countries, however, tend to deemphasize and even avoid instructional supervision, upholding the belief that teachers should be allowed to act individually, in accordance with their own teaching experience and discretion. Our recent study clearly illustrated the negative influence of low power distance on principals' direct instructional leadership in this domain.

As explained by Anne, an experienced high school principal: "I give my teachers wide latitude so that they can do their teaching job as they know best. Otherwise, I would simply be distrusting them." More broadly, principals gave only limited guidance on what needed to be taught, when it should be taught, and how it should be taught (i.e., coordinating the curriculum, monitoring student progress—see Table 1).

Classroom observations were similarly perceived as problematic by these principals facing a low power distance culture. Alfred, with eight years of experience as an elementary school principal, avoided observations out of sensitivity to teachers' expectation that his power would be decentralized and shared rather than exerted directly, thereby illustrating the power distance: "It doesn't matter how long in advance I notify them and how I explain the goals of observations. It's the practice itself that evokes resistance in teachers."

Likewise, clearly espousing the voice of a powerful person trying to minimize hierarchy, Vivian, with 11 years of experience as a junior high school principal, chose to act as a consultant rather than an authority: "I never tell them: 'Don't teach that way!' It's always like 'If it were me, I would teach this way.'"

Low power distance also shaped the enactment of the third key element of instructional leadership, described by Hallinger and Murphy (1985) as the major dimension of *Developing a Positive School Learning Climate*.

For example, when outlining their role definition, principals did not include behaviors such as setting boundaries or expectations for how teachers should take full advantage of potential instructional time. Alma, with two years of experience as a high school principal, admitted honestly: "Sometimes I see how my teachers go back late to their classrooms after a break. I know they missed almost 10 minutes, but I say nothing."

Low power distance also impacted the fourth key element of instructional leadership, described as *Developing Teachers* (Hallinger & Murphy, 1985) or more generally as *Developing People* (Leithwood & Louis, 2011) in the school (see Table 1). Nurturing teachers' professional growth is clearly a main function of instructional leaders.

However, principals operating in a low power distance context found it difficult to get their teachers to participate in structured professional learning activities. Joel, with 12 years of experience as an elementary school principal, openly articulated the low power distance: "I am required to make sure that teachers develop professionally but, in point of fact, if a teacher doesn't want to—she won't go."

The principals also refrained from wielding their authority to make participation mandatory in the professional development activities of the school. Instead, they relied on persuasion and encouragement to promote teachers' participation in further learning pursuits. While the interviewed principals noted that their attempts were not always successful, this was accepted as part and parcel of the existing power relationships within the school context. Thus, even when unsuccessful, the principals did not view the use of "position power" as appropriate for obtaining teacher participation.

Similarly, principals faced difficulties in applying their responsibility as an instructional leader to promote *Redesigning of the Organization,* an instructional leadership practice identified by Leithwood and Louis (2011; see Table 1). For example, Leo, with four years of experience as an elementary school principal, wanted his school to move to a block schedule, which would organize the school day into fewer but longer class periods so as to permit more flexibility for instructional activities.

However, he was disappointed with his lack of success: "I'm still convinced that this is the right step, but we [the teachers and I] were in disagreement, and I couldn't force my mindset on them." Both the teachers' openly vehement expression of opposition to the suggested school change and Leo's feeling that he could not impose his opinion on them expressed the low power distance.

It is interesting to note that, in parallel, low power distance was equally evident in the surprisingly low level of principals' commitment to meeting superintendents' instructional leadership demands. For example, the principals knew that they were expected to demonstrate instructional leadership as defined by national Ministry of Education policy. Yet, mirroring their own relationships with teachers, the principals believed that their approach to leadership could not be dictated from above. Therefore, even in the face of pressures from above, they tended to rely on their own professional judgment (see Chapter 12 for more on principals' boundary management).

CONCLUSION

This chapter illustrates how schools' national context may influence principals' implementation of instructional leadership. Particularly, as a case in point, this chapter shows how low power distance—both between principals and their subordinates and between principals and their supervisors—serves as a factor that inhibits instructional leadership. This case exemplifies the complexity of policy borrowing.

By drawing upon policy solutions that "worked" in another society, in this case solutions that worked in the United States, the borrowed policies may have been expected to incur a smaller risk, reduce uncertainty, and shorten the planning process. However, borrowed policies are not free of limitations. Failure to take into account the complex characteristics of each national context may result in resistance, partial implementation, and unanticipated outcomes.

The prominently defiant stance on the part of principals toward their superiors in our study—indicative of the national low power distance context—may provide important insight into some of the reasons underlying these principals' inadequate implementation of instructional leadership despite the steadfast calls by policymakers, researchers, and principal educators to apply this leadership approach. Further accumulation of qualitative empirical findings regarding other countries having low or high-power distance structures would enable better identification of the mechanisms underlying less successful cross-cultural policy borrowing.

PRACTICAL RECOMMENDATIONS ON INSTRUCTIONAL LEADERSHIP APPLICATION IN LOW POWER DISTANCE CONTEXTS FOR POLICYMAKERS, PRINCIPAL EDUCATORS, SUPERINTENDENTS, AND PRINCIPALS

- In countries characterized by low power distance, where the society finds it difficult to accept that power is unevenly distributed among people, principals should find ways to implement the main functions of

instructional leadership nonetheless. Support from superintendents can be very helpful.
- Integrating the norm of low power distance with the authoritative aspects of instructional leadership can be based on a paradoxical approach (see Chapter 11).
- A specific version of instructional leadership should be developed for each national context, which preserves the essence of instructional leadership—the principal's ongoing participation in improving teaching and curriculum—but also considers the national context's values and norms.

REFERENCES

Aas, M., & Brandmo, C. (2016). Revisiting instructional and transformational leadership: The contemporary Norwegian context of school leadership. *Journal of Educational Administration, 54*(1), 92–110.

Bowers, A. J. (2020). *Examining a congruency-typology model of leadership for learning using two-level latent class analysis with TALIS 2018*. OECD Publishing.

Clarke, S., & O'Donoghue, T. (2017). Educational leadership and context: A rendering of an inseparable relationship. *British Journal of Educational Studies, 65*(2), 167–182.

Hallinger, P. (2018). Bringing context out of the shadows of leadership. *Educational Management Administration & Leadership, 46*(1), 5–24.

Hallinger, P., & Murphy, J. (1985). Assessing the instructional management behavior of principals. *The Elementary School Journal, 86*(2), 217–247.

Hofstede, G. (2001). *Culture's consequences: Comparing values, behaviors, institutions and organizations across nations* (2nd ed.). Sage.

Leithwood, K., & Louis, K. S. (2011). *Linking leadership to student learning*. Jossey Bass.

Ng, F. S. D., Nguyen, T. D., Wong, K. S. B., & Choy, K. W. W. (2015). Instructional leadership practices in Singapore. *School Leadership & Management, 35*(4), 388–407.

Nir, A. E., Kondakci, Y., & Emil, S. (2018). Travelling policies and contextual considerations: On threshold criteria. *Compare: A Journal of Comparative and International Education, 48*(1), 21–38.

Pan, H. L. W., Nyeu, F. Y., & Cheng, S. H. (2017). Leading school for learning: Principal practices in Taiwan. *Journal of Educational Administration, 55*(2), 168–185.

Qian, H., Walker, A., & Li, X. (2017). The west wind vs. the east wind: Instructional leadership model in China. *Journal of Educational Administration, 55*(2), 186–206.

Shaked, H., Benoliel, P., & Hallinger, P. (2020). How national context indirectly influences instructional leadership implementation: The case of Israel. *Educational Administration Quarterly, 57*(3), 437–469.

Steiner-Khamsi, G. (2016). New directions in policy borrowing research. *Asia Pacific Education Review, 17*(3), 381–390.

Chapter 7

Inhibitors of Instructional Leadership Application in Rural Education

ABSTRACT

Considering that school leadership is context dependent, the exploration of contextual influences on instructional leadership application is most needed. As a case in point, this chapter presents research on factors that may inhibit instructional leadership application in rural schools. Specifically, rural principals assert that they should refrain from practicing instructional leadership because of two specific inhibiting factors: relationships within the community, which make it difficult for them to implement a school leadership policy that includes monitoring and control, and characteristics of parents, who disagree with the instructional leadership's emphasis on learning and achievement. Practical suggestions about applying instructional leadership in rural areas complete the chapter.

RURAL PRINCIPALSHIP

As seen in previous chapters, school leadership is inherently shaped by numerous aspects of the school context. Therefore, the principal role should not be explored through the lens of a generic set of leadership principles alone; instead, contextual features must also be taken into account (Miller, 2018). However, to date, little empirical research has explored school leadership from a perspective that emphasizes sensitivity to contextual power (Clarke & O'Donoghue, 2017).

In too many cases, the school leadership literature focuses on "what works" in general, rather than on "what works in a specific context" (Hallinger, 2018). To help address this lacuna in the literature, my recent study (Shaked, in press) sought to examine possible factors that may inhibit instructional leadership application (see Chapter 4) in the specific geo-social context of rural educational systems.

In many countries around the globe, education in rural regions is often relatively inferior compared to urban regions (e.g., Corbett & Gereluk, 2020; Cuervo, 2016; du Plessis & Mestry, 2019; Glover et al., 2016; Yue et al., 2018). Rural school principals face a wide range of predominant challenges (Preston et al., 2013).

For one, children in rural areas often enter school with less advanced academic skills than children in non-rural areas (Miller & Votruba-Drzal, 2013). Children's motivation as students is also frequently lower (Hardré & Hennessey, 2010), as is their confidence that they will still be attending school several years later (Snyder et al., 2009).

It is also difficult to recruit and retain good teaching staff in rural regions (Lock et al., 2012). Teachers in rural schools are often insufficiently trained (Monk, 2007). They do not have enough opportunities to participate in meaningful professional development (Glover et al., 2016), and their access to instructional technology is often more limited than in urban regions (Howley et al., 2011).

Moreover, rural principals see themselves as less autonomous than non-rural principals (Beesley & Clark, 2015). In all, these common challenges may explain the higher principal turnover rates noted in rural districts than in other districts (Hansen, 2018).

Significantly, rural principals' instructional leadership may be influenced by the principal-teacher relationships characterizing rural schools, which are based on close, warm interpersonal connections (Lock et al., 2012; Preston & Barnes, 2017; Wallin & Newton, 2013).

Rural principals prefer a relational leadership style along with care-focused decision making. They express a need to prioritize caring for teachers' well-being, employing a "power with" instead of "power over" leadership structure (Bartling, 2013). Rural principals stress their importance as sources of support for teachers, buffering external constraints placed on effective learning and assessment. They uphold that instructional leadership is best practiced when managed collegially rather than bureaucratically because the bureaucratic environment is incompatible with rural professional contexts' familial nature (Renihan & Noonan, 2012). They believe that informal, impromptu meetings with teachers are precious for understanding their staff's professional development needs (Cortez-Jiminez, 2012). By the same token, rural principals are seen by teachers as more accessible than their urban counterparts (Preston, 2012).

Rural principals' relationships with parents and communities are also significant. For rural principals, communication and involvement with parents and the community are essential (Latham et al., 2014). Rural principals see the enjoyment of having close relationships with the local community as a positive feature, even if dealing with community tensions and assuming community leadership roles are considered daunting (Lock et al., 2012).

Rural communities expect principals to be visible at school and in the community, whether they reside in the community or not. This visibility means that the principals are essentially "on the job" at all times, serving as role models. As such, the principals realize that their behaviors and those of their own family members need to meet community members' expectations and fit the professional role of a school principal (Bartling, 2013). Also, such expectations placed upon rural principals, to be visible and engaged, may cause them to struggle in balancing their professional and private lives (Wieczorek & Manard, 2018).

According to Preston and Barnes (2017), successful rural principals promote people-centered leadership and nurture interpersonal relationships with teachers, parents, students, and community stakeholders. Against this backdrop, my recent study (Shaked, in press) sought to identify if the unique student and teacher characteristics, interpersonal dynamics, and community expectations from rural principals' work would inhibit some aspects of these school leaders' instructional leadership application.

Chapter 4 above discussed several inhibitory factors of instructional leadership application (Shaked, 2019): limited available time, poor pedagogical knowledge, deeply rooted organizational norms, and inhibitory perceptions regarding principal-teacher relationships, the principal's role, and the goal of schooling. Chapters 5 and 6 above highlighted the additional inhibitory impact of contextual factors like clan culture and low power distance.

Further qualitative data analysis from Shaked (in press) revealed that rural principals mentioned two additional explanations for why they only apply instructional leadership to a limited extent. These two inhibitors of instructional leadership application—relationships within the community and parents' characteristics—were related to the rural context within which their school leadership took place, as presented next.

Relationships Within the Community

One reason voiced by rural principals to explain why they only partially applied instructional leadership was their belief that the principal-teacher relationship required for this type of results-based leadership was inappropriate to the intimacy and size of their small community. These principals asserted that rural schools need a friendly, collegial atmosphere, whereas they viewed instructional leadership as involving a more controlling atmosphere and formal monitoring behaviors on their part.

Principals claimed that "everything is less formal" in rural areas (James, with eight years of experience as an elementary school principal). Esther, with 15 years of experience as an elementary school principal, said that in her school "There is less emphasis on established authority figures or multiple levels of hierarchy. Rather, authority is equal among all staff members." Elaine, with seven years of experience as a junior high school principal, asserted: "Finding the right balance of informality and professionalism can be tricky. The informality creates a pleasant atmosphere, but sometimes I feel that the price paid by reduced professionalism is too high."

This study's interviewed principals also underscored that in rural communities, the principal and teachers were neighbors in a small locality and had known each other for many years. Thus, there were limits to the authority that the principal could exercise. Karen, with two years of experience as a high school principal, explained: "I meet the teachers not only at school but also at the grocery store, the playground, and the swimming pool. Our relationship cannot be only professional."

Similarly, with two years of experience as an elementary school principal, Kimberly said: "I won't be a principal here forever. And I will have to live with these teachers in the same community for many years to come. There are some things I just can't do."

Rural principals argued that because of their community's characteristics, they could not force their opinion on their teachers. For example, Dorothy, with four years of experience as an elementary school principal, shared: "It is very difficult for me to introduce changes in curriculum and teaching methods if the teachers oppose them."

Likewise, Charles, with five years of experience as a high school principal, complained: "I can't force my instructional goals on them. I have to compromise." Barbara, with 16 years of experience as an elementary school principal, related: "They don't always understand that in the end, I'm supposed to be leading the school's instructional direction. They expect me to be the one who adapts."

From principals' point of view, one particularly difficult challenge stemming from their school climate's emphasis on interpersonal relationships involved the need to conduct close supervision of teachers' work, as required under instructional leadership. With 14 years of experience as a junior high school principal, Patricia argued that classroom observations were especially problematic in her school: "From the teachers' perspective, my observing them means that I don't trust or appreciate them, which is insulting to them. So I avoid observations."

Sharon, with eight years of experience as an elementary school principal, found it challenging to evaluate teachers properly: "Teachers expect me to give high ratings in teacher evaluation, even to those teachers who are less effective. In their view, even if there are problems, I shouldn't report them. Teachers' livelihoods must not be threatened."

Characteristics of Parents and Community

Another major reason rural principals reported applying instructional leadership only to a limited extent was their sense that instructional leadership's priorities did not match the preferences of their students' parents. From the interviewed rural principals' perspective, instructional leaders should place student learning and achievements at the top of their priority list, but parents ascribed less importance to these issues.

According to these rural principals, the parents of their students did not see academic achievement as a matter of paramount importance and, therefore, did not want their children to feel overloaded by academic pressures. Principals described rural parents who argued that: "There are too many requirements" (Bob, with 16 years of experience as a high school principal); "Children are constantly barraged with educational expectations to be met" (Carol, with 11 years of experience as a junior high school principal); "Kids have no downtime at all. They can't go outside and play because of the amount of homework they have to do" (John, with 16 years of experience as an elementary school principal).

The principals in my recent study claimed that rural parents do not attach importance to academic results because it does not matter to them whether their children continue to higher education. With 15 years of experience as a high school principal, Gloria said: "Quite a few parents here do not have academic degrees, nor is it imperative to them that their children get academic degrees." Similarly, Deborah, with six years of experience as an elementary school principal, said: "They are not the type of parents who aspire for their children to work in prestigious professions, such as engineers or high-tech workers. It does not really interest them."

According to rural principals, teachers at rural schools are part of the community, and therefore they often hold views similar to those of the students' parents. Sandra, with four years of experience as an elementary school principal, said: "When I bring up for discussion the claims of parents that students should not be pressured too much, some teachers agree with them. Not only do our parents fail to attach much importance to academic success, but some of the teaching staff also feel the same way."

Similarly, Linda, with 13 years of experience as an elementary school principal, said: "I used to work in the center of the country, and I can see that the teachers here in the periphery have a different perception of their role. They do not let students work hard." Importantly, this perspective gearing principals away from instructional leadership targets seemed to pervade not only the parents and school staff but even principals' own supervisors.

For example, Margaret, with two years of experience as an elementary school principal, heard a similar lackadaisical position from the education department head in her school's local municipal authority: "Many municipal heads pressure principals to show rapid improvement in student achievements, but in our region we get the message that it's not really of any interest."

Interestingly, some of the interviewed rural principals agreed, at least to some extent, with parents' and teachers' attitude that there was no need for students to invest in intensive study and the pursuit of high grades. Moreover, such principals believed that they needed to tailor their school leadership priorities to the expectations of the school community. For example, Monica, with 19 years of experience as a high school principal, explained: "Principalship needs to adapt to the community it serves. You can't go against the parents. That is why my school pays a lot of attention to extracurricular activities and not just learning and outcomes."

Conclusion

Schools' contextual effects on instructional leadership application are worthy of academic attention. This chapter aimed to identify the factors inhibiting instructional leadership application that characterize schools in rural areas in order to better contextualize previous findings on inhibitors.

As mentioned in Chapter 4, organizational norms are one of the reasons instructional leadership fails to gain a solid foothold in the role of principals. In addition, principals' fear that instructional leadership could damage principal-teacher relationships was found to be a perception that inhibits instructional leadership application. Principals' belief that school's primary task should be a non-academic one was also identified as a perception that inhibits instructional leadership application. However, these findings were not context specific.

My recent study (Shaked, in press) complemented those findings by showing that rural principals refrain from applying this leadership style because of two inhibiting factors directly related to the nature of the rural regions in which they work. The first factor inhibiting instructional leadership application in rural schools is the principals' belief that instructional leadership requires a principal-teacher relationship that is incompatible with their relatively small community's friendly nature. The second factor inhibiting instructional leadership application in rural schools is the principals' sense that the imposed instructional leadership principles differ from the priorities upheld by their students' parents.

By linking the abovementioned inhibiting factors of instructional leadership application to cultural values and geographically informed patterns, this chapter refines the previous decontextualized explanations for how organizational norms and principals' perceptions shape the contours of principal leadership practice. Placing organizational norms and principals' perceptions in the broader context of societal norms and perceptions provides enhanced theoretical leverage.

To be noted, this chapter paints a disappointing picture of an uneducated and disadvantaged population and even unmotivated school and municipal leaders. Further research with more participants and additional rural areas may yield less pessimistic findings in terms of hopes for children to obtain more education than their parents, to learn skills that can serve them in gainful employment, or to escape the cycle of poverty.

PRACTICAL RECOMMENDATIONS ON INSTRUCTIONAL LEADERSHIP APPLICATION IN RURAL AREAS FOR POLICYMAKERS, PRINCIPAL EDUCATORS, SUPERINTENDENTS, AND PRINCIPALS

- Principals should apply instructional leadership while considering the school context, because it is not a one-size-fits-all framework. Customized versions of instructional leadership could be needed across different contexts.
- Rural principals should be especially supported by their supervisors to steadfastly apply instructional leadership, including its components that involve monitoring and evaluation, despite the friendly nature of small communities. To do this, rural principals should combine supervision of teacher practices and monitoring of student results with healthy principal-teacher relationships (see Chapter 11 regarding the paradoxical approach).
- Rural principals should strive for high achievements, even if for parents it is not very important. Sharing rationales with parents and clarifying potential benefits of students' learning and achievements for the child and the family may help encourage parents to increase their involvement and sense of ownership over the process of facilitating their children's progress in school.

REFERENCES

Bartling, E. M. (2013). *Female high school principals in rural Midwestern school districts: Their lived experiences in leadership* (Unpublished doctoral dissertation). University of Wisconsin at Milwaukee.

Beesley, A. D., & Clark, T. F. (2015). How rural and non-rural principals differ in high plains US states. *Peabody Journal of Education, 90*(2), 242–249.

Clarke, S., & O'Donoghue, T. (2017). Educational leadership and context: A rendering of an inseparable relationship. *British Journal of Educational Studies, 65*(2), 167–182.

Corbett, M., & Gereluk, D. (Eds.). (2020). *Rural teacher education: Connecting land and people.* Springer.

Cortez-Jiminez, G. (2012). *Leadership needs of California rural school administrators* (Unpublished doctoral dissertation). San Diego State University.

Cuervo, H. (2016). *Understanding social justice in rural education.* Springer.

du Plessis, P., & Mestry, R. (2019). Teachers for rural schools: A challenge for South Africa. *South African Journal of Education, 39*(4), S1–S9.

Glover, T. A., Nugent, G. C., Chumney, F. L., Ihlo, T., Shapiro, E. S., Guard, K., Koziol, N., & Bovaird, J. (2016). Investigating rural teachers' professional development, instructional knowledge, and classroom practice. *Journal of Research in Rural Education, 31*(3), 1–16.

Hallinger, P. (2018). Bringing context out of the shadows of leadership. *Educational Management Administration & Leadership, 46*(1), 5–24.

Hansen, C. (2018). Why rural principals leave. *Rural Educator, 39*(1), 41–53.

Hardré, P., & Hennessey, M. (2010). Two rural worlds: Differences of rural high school students' motivational profiles in Indiana and Colorado. *Journal of Research in Rural Education, 25*(8).

Howley, A., Wood, L., & Hough, B. (2011). Rural elementary school teachers' technology integration. *Journal of Research in Rural Education, 26*(9), 1–13.

Latham, D., Smith, L. F., & Wright, K. A. (2014). Context, curriculum, and community matter: Leadership practices of primary school principals in the Otago province of New Zealand. *Rural Educator, 36*(1), n1.

Lock, G., Budgen, F., Lunay, R., & Oakley, G. (2012). The loneliness of the long-distance principal: Tales from remote Western Australia. *Australian and International Journal of Rural Education, 22*(2), 65–77.

Miller, P. W. (2018). School leadership is context dependent. In *The nature of school leadership* (pp. 121–142). Palgrave Macmillan.

Miller, P., & Votruba-Drzal, E. (2013). Early academic skills and childhood experiences across the rural-urban continuum. *Early Childhood Research Quarterly, 28*(2), 234–248.

Monk, D. H. (2007). Recruiting and retaining high-quality teachers in rural areas. *The Future of Children, 17*(1), 155–174.

Preston, J. P. (2012). Rural and urban teaching experiences: Narrative expressions. *Alberta Journal Educational Research, 58*(1), 41–57.

Preston, J. P., & Barnes, K. E. (2017). Successful leadership in rural schools: Cultivating collaboration. *Rural Educator, 38*(1), 6–15.

Preston, J. P., Jakubiec, B. A., & Kooymans, R. (2013). Common challenges faced by rural principals: A review of the literature. *The Rural Educator, 35*(1).

Renihan, P., & Noonan, B. (2012). Principals as assessment leaders in rural schools. *The Rural Educator, 33*(3), 1–8.

Shaked, H. (2019). Perceptual inhibitors of instructional leadership in Israeli principals. *School Leadership & Management, 39*(5), 519–536.

Shaked, H. (in press). Between center and periphery: Instructional leadership in Israeli rural schools. *International Journal of Educational Management.*

Snyder, A., McLaughlin, D., & Coleman-Jensen, A. (2009). *The new, longer road to adulthood: Schooling, work, and idleness among rural youth.* University of New Hampshire.

Wallin, D., & Newton, P. (2013). Instructional leadership of the rural teaching principal: Double the trouble or twice the fun? *International Studies in Educational Administration (Commonwealth Council for Educational Administration & Management [CCEAM]), 41*(2), 19–31.

Wieczorek, D., & Manard, C. (2018). Instructional leadership challenges and practices of novice principals in rural schools. *Journal of Research in Rural Education, 34*(2).

Yue, A., Tang, B., Shi, Y., Tang, J., Shang, G., Medina, A., & Rozelle, S. (2018). Rural education across China's 40 years of reform: Past successes and future challenges. *China Agricultural Economic Review, 10*(1), 93–118.

PART III

Incomplete Application of Instructional Leadership

This part of the book closely examines situations in which instructional leadership tends to be applied only partially. Chapter 8 clarifies why principals tend to turn teacher evaluation into a useless component of instructional leadership. Chapter 9 explains why the vital task of ensuring that the "right" teachers are on staff is rarely seen as an inherent component of instructional leadership. Finally, Chapter 10 concentrates on the boundaries of instructional leadership in assistant principals, who are considered in the research literature to be "forgotten leaders."

PART III

Incomplete Application of Instructional Leadership

Chapter 8

Principals' Incomplete Performance of Teacher Evaluation

ABSTRACT

Whether due to insufficient enablers or excessive inhibitors, principals tend to apply instructional leadership incompletely in particular situations. A case in point is teacher evaluation—an essential component of instructional leadership. Recent research found that principals who are required to evaluate their teachers often give higher ratings than what they think these teachers deserve. This chapter presents four considerations of school principals that lead to teachers' over-evaluation and therefore their inadequate implementation of instructional leadership: (1) time constraints/prioritization (low perceived value for high time investment); (2) evaluation's ineffectiveness for improving teaching (via teacher development or dismissal); (3) the imprecision of teacher evaluation measurements; and (4) impingement on interpersonal relationships. The chapter concludes by offering practical recommendations related to principals' unsatisfactory performance of teacher evaluation.

A LONG-STANDING FAILURE TO RECOGNIZE VARIATIONS IN TEACHER EFFECTIVENESS

To meet instructional leaders' major expected goal of focusing their efforts directly onto promoting the best teaching practices in their schools, the accurate evaluation of teachers should be among principals' core activities. In general, teacher evaluation has two basic purposes: measuring teachers and developing teachers (Marzano, 2012). Teacher measurement discerns differences between various teachers' levels of effectiveness, while teacher development provides teachers with meaningful feedback about their practice in order to bring about improved instruction and achievement.

However, an increasing body of research has indicated that teacher evaluation by principals actually fails to provide reliable information regarding teacher quality because teachers almost always receive high ratings from their principals. Toch and Rothman (2008) discovered that 87% of the 600 schools in the Chicago school system did not rate even one teacher as unsatisfactory even though 10% of those schools were classified as "failing educationally" (Marzano & Toth, 2013, p. 2). The rating scale used in Chicago included four grades: superior, excellent, satisfactory, and unsatisfactory. Yet, overall, only 0.3% of Chicago's 25,000 teachers were rated as unsatisfactory, while 93% of teachers in the system were rated as "superior" or "excellent" (New Teacher Project, 2007).

Similarly, Weisberg and colleagues' (2009) research, which was based on survey responses from approximately 15,000 teachers and 1,300 administrators from four U.S. states, showed that in districts that used binary satisfactory/unsatisfactory ratings, virtually all tenured teachers (more than 99%) received the satisfactory rating. The number receiving an unsatisfactory rating amounted to a fraction of a percentage. In districts that used a broader range of rating options, 70% of tenured teachers received the highest rating, and another 24% received the second-highest rating. Weisberg and his colleagues called this phenomenon "the Widget Effect" (p. 4):

> The Widget Effect describes the tendency of school districts to assume classroom effectiveness is the same from teacher to teacher. This decades-old fallacy fosters an environment in which teachers cease to be understood as individual professionals, but rather as interchangeable parts.

Weisberg and his colleagues (2009) further demonstrated that these inflated formal teacher ratings did not reflect evaluators' actual ability to recognize differences in teachers' effectiveness. They found that a high percentage of principals and teachers (81% and 57%, respectively) could identify a poorly performing teacher in their school, despite the fact that in most districts less than 1% of teachers were given a formal unsatisfactory rating.

More recently, Kraft and Gilmour (2017) revisited these findings in 24 states that had adopted large-scale reforms in their teacher-evaluation methods. Although the full distribution of ratings was found to vary widely across states, with 0.7% to 28.7% of teachers rated as below proficient and 6% to 62% rated as above proficient, the percentage of teachers rated as unsatisfactory remained as before, at less than 1% in the vast majority of states.

To better understand why principals may decide to over-evaluate the teachers in their employ, thereby missing out on a crucial tool for implementing effective instructional leadership, I conducted a qualitative empirical research study analyzing diverse school principals' perceptions and concerns on the matter of teacher evaluation. This study (Shaked, 2018) identified four main considerations that principals take into account, which might lead them to give higher evaluations than what the principals think their teachers really deserve: (1) time constraints/prioritization (low perceived value for the needed large investment of time); (2) evaluation's ineffectiveness for improving teaching (by leading to teacher development or dismissal); (3) the imprecision of teacher evaluation measurements; and (4) impingement on interpersonal relationships. Although these four considerations were distinct, they were closely interrelated within principals' processes of teacher evaluation.

Time Constraints and Prioritization

Principals' most frequent reason for giving higher ratings than what they thought teachers deserved was their sense of time constraints surrounding the evaluation process. According to principals, the teacher evaluation procedure is a multi-step process demanding a substantial chunk of the time that they need to devote to school management. Inasmuch as principals perceived themselves as lacking the intensive amounts of uninterrupted time required, they reported performing the evaluation procedure only partially.

As a result of their insufficient time to complete a comprehensive evaluation, principals felt the need to inflate teachers' ratings, "just to be on the safe side" or "to be fair." One principal's description illustrates this link between inadequate time for accurate evaluation and inflated ratings (Naomi, with nine years of experience as an elementary school principal): "The teacher evaluation procedure takes about nine meetings. That is simply too much. I wish I had that time. I have no free time, nor do I have control over how I spend my time." Therefore, Naomi shared how she coped with these time constraints: "So, I do the procedure very partially, give the teacher a high rating so that she won't have any complaints, and thus save myself all that trouble."

However, for many principals who attributed their rating inflation to time constraints, this reason did not stand alone but rather was linked inexorably with principals' perceptions about the ineffectiveness or even uselessness of the evaluation process (see next theme), which led to these principals' low prioritization for fitting the full teacher evaluation process into their time schedule. Principals certainly do lack sufficient available time; yet the attribution of rating inflation tendencies to time constraints seemed to stem from principals' belief that teacher evaluation failed to make the best use of principals' precious time. If principals had considered teacher evaluation as making a significant contribution to their primary instructional leadership objective of improving teaching quality, they would have found time for it.

This attitude was expressed by Dennis, with nine years of experience as an elementary school principal, who admitted: "I don't invest in this nonsense, which only takes my time and does not contribute anything to the school." Similarly, Alice, with nine years of experience as an elementary school principal, asserted: "It takes a lot of time, which could be used for much more beneficial things."

These utterances illustrate how principals' low prioritization of completing a full and accurate teacher evaluation was determined simultaneously both by actual lack of time and by their perception that the needed time investment would be disproportionate to the process's potential for real, relevant effects on improving teaching quality, as presented next.

Evaluation's Ineffectiveness for Improving Teaching

The second consideration disclosed by principals as leading to teacher over-evaluation involved their perception of the required teacher evaluation process as ineffectual for improving actual instruction in the school. These principals clarified that because evaluation is not conducive to actually improving teachers' work, they saw no need to provide accurate ratings and thus took the easier path and simply gave teachers high ratings.

For example, Patricia, with 11 years of experience as an elementary school principal, claimed that the required evaluation was not an effective way to improve the quality of teachers' work: "I give teachers high ratings because this procedure [of teacher evaluation] focuses only on giving teachers a performance score. A teacher does not become an expert as a result of being evaluated, so I save my time for improvement programs." According to Patricia, inasmuch as the standard evaluation process is not accompanied by an improvement plan that includes support for teachers' professional development, there is no point in investing effort into it.

Some principals felt that evaluations could contribute nothing new to veteran teachers. A number of principals articulated the belief that evaluations could not make any impact because "people do not change" (Ashley, with 23 years of experience as an elementary school principal) or "since they don't really want to make the change deep down, it will be very hard to go the distance" (Helen, with seven years of experience as an elementary school principal).

Other principals pinpointed the ineffectuality of teacher evaluation due to teacher tenure policy, which restricts principals' ability to fire teachers. These principals claimed that because tenured teachers' dismissal is not feasible, the results of low teacher evaluation can yield no significant usefulness. For example, Bonnie, with eight years of experience as an elementary school principal, said: "Tenure makes removal of poorly performing teachers, who have actually been found in their evaluation to be ineffective in the classroom, simply impossible. If evaluation is impotent, why should I give real scores?" Bonnie's remarks highlighted that for tenured poorly performing teachers who could not be fired, an honest evaluation would only increase tension in the workplace.

Donald, with 12 years of experience as an elementary school principal, one of only two interviewed principals who claimed that despite all odds they always gave teachers the exact ratings they deserved, also expressed frustration with the tenure policy. Donald explained: "I rate teachers as I think they really deserve because, in my eyes, this is my professionalism as a principal. Does it help? Not really, because it is too difficult to get rid of a bad teacher."

Importantly, several principals' explanations for their inflation of teacher ratings revealed that—in stark contrast to experts' and their superiors' steadfast recommendations to embrace instructional leadership—these principals simply did not view the improvement of their school's quality of instruction as a central component of their principalship role. Such principals explicitly asserted that teacher evaluation is pointless because principals are not expected to deal with improving teaching quality.

For example, Jose, with 13 years of experience as an elementary school principal, argued: "I'm no longer a teacher, and I'm not in the teaching business now. The teachers know how to do their job, and my job is to make sure they have the conditions to succeed."

The Imprecision of Teacher Evaluation Measurements

The third reason described for the frequent inflation of teacher ratings was principals' perception that teacher evaluation methods cannot yield a complete, accurate picture of teachers' actual quality and real-time functioning on the ground. Asserting that instruction is too complicated to be measured accurately, many interviewed principals reported that they would often raise ratings beyond what teachers deserved because they believed that teacher evaluation could not be performed in a way that precisely represented all relevant details about the teacher's quality.

Several principals claimed that reliable teacher measurement is hindered by the existence of numerous, multiple paths that can reach the ultimate goal of effective teaching. For example, Harry, with nine years of experience as an elementary school principal, explained: "Great teachers do make a difference, but that doesn't mean they all do so in the same way. The evaluation system assumes that all the great teachers look the same, but this is not the case in reality." This view of teachers' desired qualifications and assets as too indefinable to quantify or prioritize coincides with the findings presented below (in Chapter 9) in the context of how to select the "right" teachers for the job.

In addition to the complexity of determining who is a good teacher, principals believed that the evaluation of teachers' desired characteristics should also take the specific educational context into account. Heather, with seven years of experience as an elementary school principal, said: "Exemplary teaching looks and sounds different across different classrooms. We should lift our eyes up from the list of indices and see whether classroom practice actually reflects the education we want for our students."

Focusing on one example of contextual factors that should affect teacher evaluation, Kenneth, with 14 years of experience as a junior high school principal, discussed the differing characteristics necessary for rural versus urban schools: "I believe that schools in the countryside are substantially different. While residents of metropolitan areas are competitive and look mainly for results, our parents have other priorities. Therefore, we need different teachers." (See Chapter 7 for more on the rural versus urban distinction.)

In sum, principals perceived the standard teacher evaluation measurements at their disposal to be ambiguous and generic rather than precise and context specific. Considering the evaluation process to be untrustworthy, principals gave teachers overly high ratings to leave a safety margin in case the evaluation methods were imprecise and to ensure fairness for their teachers whose qualities and fit to the current learning context may not have been accurately captured.

Impingement on Interpersonal Relationships

The final, fourth reason for often giving teachers high ratings was a familiar consideration, discussed previously in this book: the desire to maintain positive relationships with teachers. Principals feared that giving poor ratings could harm their good relations with teachers, especially because principals considered their good working and personal relationships to be crucial for school improvement efforts.

Jason, with 10 years of experience as an elementary school principal, articulated this view clearly: "My good relationship with teachers allows me to run the school successfully. I work hard to build such relationships and do not want teacher evaluation to spoil it." Walter, with six years of experience as a junior high school principal, emphasized his school's positive atmosphere, which allowed no room for the conflict inherent to serious teacher criticism: "If I were to give a tough teacher evaluation like I was asked to do, it might damage the positive atmosphere we have."

For such principals, teacher evaluation is not just pointless because of its ineffectuality; it may even be considered an active hindrance to school work. Linda, with 16 years of experience as a junior high school principal, gave voice to this argument: "Teachers should not be under a magnifying glass.

Evaluation is stressful for the teachers, and therefore not only does it not improve their work but, to the contrary, it harms it. I conduct teacher evaluation because I have to, but to minimize the damage, I always give teachers high ratings to relieve the pressure stemming from this process." In addition, often having a close personal or even familial affiliation with their teachers, principals did not want low ratings to prevent those teachers' promotion to a higher salary level.

Thus, interpersonal relationships were a priority for some of the principals not only because of the importance attributed to principal-teacher relationships for school success but also because of principals' warm, long-term relationships with their teachers. (To be noted, the connections between interpersonal relationships and instructional leadership application are mentioned in many chapters of this book.) Altogether, principals' over-evaluation of teachers took into account the risk of low ratings' deleterious impact on highly valued principal-teacher relationships and on the less proficient teachers themselves who, even when not functioning optimally, were nonetheless close friends.

CONCLUSION

Teacher evaluation should be a major component of instructional leadership application in order to measure teachers' ongoing functioning in the school and to tailor teachers' professional development based on evaluation outputs. However, researchers have found that principals very often give their teachers the highest possible ratings and only in rare cases evaluate their poorly performing teachers as unsatisfactory (Kraft & Gilmour, 2017; Toch & Rothman, 2008). Such skewed ratings do not allow for discrimination between effective and ineffective teachers and do not provide high-quality feedback to improve teachers' functioning as effective educators (Marzano & Toth, 2013; Weisberg et al., 2009), thus seriously hampering instructional leadership successes.

My study (Shaked, 2018) identified four considerations of principals who give their teachers overly high ratings—as related to principals' low prioritization of teacher evaluation within their time constraints, view of the evaluation process as impotent to improve teaching, perception of available evaluation methods as imprecise for measuring teachers, and concern about its negative effects on interpersonal relationships. These considerations led principals not only to avoid low ratings but also to inflate high ratings.

The inability of principals to distinguish between excellent, good, fair, and poor teaching is a violation of their role as instructional leaders. When teacher effectiveness—the most crucial factor in school improvement—is not measured, documented, or used to inform decision making in any meaningful way, principals do not adequately apply instructional leadership.

PRACTICAL RECOMMENDATIONS ON TEACHER EVALUATION FOR POLICYMAKERS, PRINCIPAL EDUCATORS, SUPERINTENDENTS, AND PRINCIPALS

- Principals should be provided with evaluation models that are based on clear and straightforward performance standards, which fairly, accurately, and credibly differentiate high- from low-performing teachers in various contexts.
- Principals should receive explicit training not only in how to measure teacher performance against predetermined standards but also in how to follow up on evaluation by furnishing teachers with constructive feedback and by supporting low-performing teachers.
- Principals should become aware of the negative consequences of giving overly high ratings in teacher evaluation so as not to harm teacher-principal relationships.
- Principals should be held accountable for evaluating teachers precisely. Their judgments should be regularly monitored.
- Principals should be allowed to require teachers to participate in mandatory professional development programs based on inadequate evaluation results.
- Principals should be given authority to determine teachers' salaries and continuation of work based on the results of teacher evaluation.

REFERENCES

Kraft, M. A., & Gilmour, A. F. (2017). Revisiting the Widget Effect: Teacher evaluation reforms and the distribution of teacher effectiveness. *Educational Researcher*, *46*(5), 234–249.

Marzano, R. J. (2012). Teacher evaluation: What's fair? What's effective? *Educational Leadership*, *70*(3), 14–19.

Marzano, R. J., & Toth, M. D. (2013). *Teacher evaluation that makes a difference: A new model for teacher growth and student achievement.* Association for Supervision and Curriculum Development.

New Teacher Project. (2007). *Hiring, assignment, and transfer in Chicago public schools.* Author.

Shaked, H. (2018). Why principals often give overly high ratings on teacher evaluations. *Studies in Educational Evaluation*, *59*, 150–157.

Toch, T., & Rothman, R. (2008). *Rush to judgment: Teacher evaluation in public education.* Education Sector.

Weisberg, D., Sexton, S., Mulhern, J., & Keeling, D. (2009). *The widget effect: Our national failure to acknowledge and act on differences in teacher effectiveness.* New Teacher Project.

Chapter 9

Principals' Incomplete Assurance of Teachers' Job Suitability

ABSTRACT

Although the frameworks of instructional leadership provided by leading scholars have generally incorporated multiple ways to improve teaching, they have not yet included the fundamental role of hiring the best available teachers and dismissing inappropriate teachers. This chapter suggests that ensuring that one's hired school staff is up to the task of achieving the desired student outcomes should be a foremost concern of instructional leaders. Yet, principals tend to perceive the issue of teacher hiring/firing as complicated. Consequently, they often regard associated human-resources tasks as impossible or impractical, such as deciding which attributes are most important for effective teachers, determining how such effective teachers can be proficiently screened for hire, and executing dismissal of ineffective ones. The chapter concludes with feasible recommendations about ensuring the job suitability of teachers.

ENSURING TEACHERS' APPROPRIATENESS

Although several frameworks describe the dimensions and components of instructional leadership (see Introduction and Table 1), surprisingly, ensuring teachers' appropriateness through personnel management is not explicitly included in those frameworks. Namely, the task of ensuring that those individual teachers in each principal's employ are in point of fact suitable for this complex and significant job has been solely neglected in the literature, despite this task's commonsense vital role as an essential component of effective instructional leadership. Thus, whereas the quality of teaching activity has received major emphasis in instructional leadership models, the quality of those actual people hired to work as teachers in schools has been virtually overlooked.

The "right" attributes for working as an effective teacher have been discussed in the literature on teachers' quality. These attributes may include (a) high intelligence or analytic ability, including the capacity to attain subject-matter expertise and to master education-related knowledge; (b) teaching skills, such as explaining ideas and concepts clearly, motivating and sustaining students' interest, using active-learning techniques, and acting as a facilitator to encourage and guide learning; (c) interpersonal skills like classroom management capability, caring, empathy, and tolerance for diversity; (d) motivation and passion for teaching; and so on (e.g., Connell, 2009; Darling-Hammond & Baratz-Snowden, 2005; Liu, 2009). Likewise, the literature has acknowledged that teachers on staff who are unintelligent, untrained, unmotivated, burnt out, and so forth are likely to be conducive to poor student achievement and may preclude staff's development and growth (e.g., Nixon et al., 2016; Winters, 2012).

Some of the studies examining teacher quality have touched upon conceptual frameworks related to fit—whether referring to person-job fit, person-organization fit, or person-group fit—that are appropriate when considering suitability (Harris et al., 2010; Ingle et al., 2011).

Others have used economic terms, with teachers' job suitability seen as representing the neoliberalism that focuses on economic efficiency, whereas the rights of workers (who may be unsuitable for the job) may be considered impediments to maximum performance. Neoliberalism is "capitalism with the gloves off" (McChesney, 2011, p. 8), meaning that neoliberalism is pure capitalism, without workers' rights and organizations. In building a capitalist society, labor commodification may be seen as a core process (Maddison, 2008).

Therefore, one may argue that when we speak about teachers as human capital rather than as human beings, they become a commodity. They are treated—at least conceptually—as things to be bought, sold, invested in, or traded. Inasmuch as an absolute majority of teachers in most countries are women, commodification and exploitation might be two sides of the same gendered coin (Mezzadri, 2016).

One of the fundamental questions regarding individual teachers' suitability for the job is whether teaching ability is inherited (innate) or learned (acquired). If good teachers are made, not born, then principals do not need to focus on determining who to hire and fire but rather can focus on expanding the abilities of any teachers currently at hand.

However, good teachers are, apparently, both born and made. We know that teaching skills can be studied, practiced, and ultimately improved. At the same time, consistent differences in teaching effectiveness within cohorts of beginning teachers emerge early and remain intact for years (Atteberry et al., 2013; Harrison et al., 2006; Wiens & Ruday, 2014).

Presumably, some individuals possess a combination of personality characteristics that are conducive to effective teaching. Nevertheless, even the most genetically blessed teacher would benefit from a teacher education program (Malikow, 2006; Scott & Dinham, 2008).

Investment of efforts into ensuring that given teachers do actually possess fundamental job suitability may be seen as contradictory to a deep belief in the capacity of all teachers to become effective. As teachers of teachers, educators in teacher preparatory training indeed must believe in the learning potential of all preservice teachers admitted into their programs. Policymakers should also remember that teaching ability can be significantly developed, as Darling-Hammond (2006, p. ix) explained:

> One of the most damaging myths prevailing in American education is the notion that good teachers are born and not made. This superstition has given rise to a set of policies that rely far too much on some kind of prenatal alchemy to produce a cadre of teachers for our nation's schools—and far too little on systematic, sustained initiatives to ensure that all teachers have the opportunity to become well prepped.

Still, to achieve the most effective schools, principals should not miss out on the opportunity to utilize hiring and firing practices as a fruitful tool for improving the quality of their school's instruction. School principals must therefore integrate, on the one hand, their belief in each teacher's ability to improve practices with, on the other hand, their ability to make courageous decisions regarding that teacher's dismissal, if warranted (Jacob, 2011; Range et al., 2012).

Despite the common sense of such an assertion, the literature to date outlining instructional leadership models (see Introduction and Table 1) has not given adequate attention to this human-resources management aspect of the principal's role. While contemporary principals are expected to be involved in a variety of activities designed to improve teachers' practices, today's principals are not necessarily expected to ensure that the "right" people—those specific human beings with the optimal characteristics for success and, crucially, those who do not possess destructive or disruptive characteristics—are those who are hired to actually teach in the classrooms, in charge of imparting knowledge and skills to students.

Beyond developing teachers, the only component found in prior instructional leadership models that could be considered relevant to the principal's role in ensuring teachers' suitability to the job is supervising, monitoring, and evaluating instruction (Hallinger & Murphy, 1985; Stronge et al., 2008). However, such supervisory and evaluative activities were conceived as aiming to provide teachers with concrete feedback on instruction itself, as explained by Robinson (2007, p. 14):

> The degree of leader involvement in classroom observation and subsequent feedback was also associated with higher performing schools. Teachers in such schools reported that their leaders set and adhered to clear performance standards for teaching and made regular classroom observations that helped them improve their teaching.

Thus, even this identified supervision-evaluation component of instructional leadership has not been typically conceptualized as aiming to help principals precisely determine whether particular teachers possess the "right" attributes to become members of the school staff or to retain their jobs over time. To address this lacuna in the prior conceptualization of instructional leaders' roles, I undertook a qualitative empirical research study investigating why this important human-resources task of principals—which holds crucial practical implications for everyday school leadership—has generally been avoided by researchers, policymakers, and teacher educators.

My recent study (Shaked, 2019) revealed that school principals perceived the issue of ensuring teacher suitability to be quite complicated—involving ambiguity, inconvenience, insufficient knowledge, and tension between advantages and disadvantages. Specifically, as seen next, my comprehensive analysis of a heterogeneous group of principals' in-depth interviews pinpointed two main areas of complexity: principals' sense of uncertainty about how to go about selecting effective teachers and the unpleasantness surrounding teacher dismissal.

Apparently, these complexities tend to lead principals to avoid human-resources tasks, to treat them as unfeasible, or to handle them intuitively rather than systematically. Unsurprisingly, considering the paucity of instructional leadership policy and research in this area, principals did not view the management of human resources to be a viable means for improving teaching and learning. Unfortunately, despite the rational logic underlying hiring and firing as crucial for establishing and maintaining a cadre of high-quality teachers, school principals in my study did not consider personnel management tasks to be an integral component of their instructional leadership role, as detailed next.

Uncertainty About Teacher Selection

Overall, principals did perceive teacher selection, screening, and hiring as having a significant impact on the quality of teaching at school, but at the same time they viewed it as an inexact multidimensional process for which they lacked knowledge, training, and confidence. They often mentioned a lack of clarity about what would be valid criteria for deciding which teacher is the "right" person to hire and about which screening methods could best identify a candidate's suitability to the job. They perceived the process of selecting new teachers as only providing limited predictive information about teachers' real-time capability on the job.

For example, Edna, with nine years of experience as a high school principal, argued: "I invest ample time and effort into teacher selection processes. However, sometimes even when you follow all the rules, you may still end up with the wrong person in the job." Similarly, Rebecca, with four years of experience as an elementary school principal, admitted: "Your seemingly perfect hire may turn out to be far from it, and you spend years dealing with the consequences."

Several possible explanations for the hiring process's limited validity were offered—some focusing on the prospective teachers and some focusing on the principal's own skills for screening job applicants. For instance, Scott, with 16 years of experience as a junior high school principal, claimed that the complexity of teacher selection stems from the fact that teachers themselves change and evolve over time: "Hiring new teachers is my best opportunity to influence the quality of my staff. However, novice teachers are inherently incapable of demonstrating high teaching ability, so you can only really get to know them after several years on the job."

Edith, with eight years of experience as an elementary school principal, provided another explanation for the complexity of teacher selection processes: "The non-cognitive attributes such as motivation, personality, resilience, and interpersonal skills, which play an important role in effective teaching, make the selection of new teachers much more challenging."

Particularly, the effectiveness of some of the common methods used by principals to evaluate teacher candidates was questioned. Rose, with four years of experience as an elementary school principal, criticized the efficiency of the customary interview procedure: "The standard interview that starts with 'So tell me about yourself' is totally worthless for predicting a candidate's capability." Kevin, with nine years of experience as an elementary school principal, noted that teacher candidates' résumés might sometimes not reflect their true abilities: "A good-looking CV is often professionally prepared, or at least professionally reviewed."

Some interviewed principals brought attention to the fact that they themselves had never undergone any systematic training that aimed explicitly to hone principals' skills for selecting new teachers effectively. With 16 years of experience as a high school principal, Betty noted: "I don't remember the superintendent ever dedicating time to this severely neglected issue."

Similarly, Bob, with 11 years of experience as a high school principal, expressed his sense that principals in general lack the needed knowledge about how to identify the right teachers: "I guess there must be many beneficial ways to hire great workers out there. We simply don't know what they are."

With regard to the broader question of "Who is a good teacher?" when considering the "right" person for an open teaching position in the school, principals emphasized the challenge and complexity involved in determining which attributes are desirable in a potential hire. Although these principals were consistently engaged in screening teacher candidates and in evaluating in-service teachers, as part and parcel of their ongoing leadership roles, many principals found it difficult to define and characterize their "preferred" teacher.

Principals' utterances revealed that part of this complexity roots in the multiple qualifications that are necessary to qualify as a "suitable" teacher. For example, Margaret, with 23 years of experience as an elementary school principal, claimed: "Good teachers are made up of a combination of hundreds of qualities. Each good teacher has her own unique mixture of these qualities." For Margaret, each good teacher is different, so that there is no one uniform definition of a good teacher.

Similarly, Michael, with seven years of experience as an elementary school principal, elaborated on some of these multiple attributes of "good" teachers: "Teaching demands a lot of qualities, such as knowledge of subject matter and curriculum, knowledge of classroom management techniques, affection for children, willingness to invest above and beyond, ability to work in a team, loyalty, and many other things. With all these required qualities, you cannot define what a good teacher is. It is very complicated." Although Michael did not mention "hundreds" of qualities like Margaret and seemed to make some attempt to weigh various expectations from teachers, Michael also agreed that the numerous merits required from teachers made it almost impossible to genuinely define one.

Like Margaret and Michael, Maria, with three years of experience as an elementary school principal, believed that the multidimensionality of teacher effectiveness makes it indefinable. In addition, importantly in the context of how instructional leadership is conceptualized, Maria, who was about to get an experienced teacher to her school, did not accept the claim that effective teachers can be recognized according to their students' results: "I don't think that student achievement could determine who is an effective teacher. An effective teacher is actually a multidimensional term, and in my opinion, it is even inconclusive."

In the face of the overwhelmingly large number of possible criteria for evaluating potential new teachers' job suitability and principals' aforementioned reported lack of training or formal knowledge in evidence-based screening procedures, some principals appeared to turn to vague instinct, gut feelings, or intuition as an intangible gauge for assessing who might be a "good" teacher:

- "The main quality I look for is a teacher who will be a kid magnet. I don't know what makes a teacher a kid magnet, but I know how to recognize it" (Sylvia, with 19 years of experience as an elementary school principal).
- "We sincerely need good teachers. However, a good teacher is not a matter of definitions. When you meet a good teacher, you know that he or she is a good teacher" (Josephine, with seven years of experience as a high school principal).
- "My hunches are formed out of my past experience and knowledge. When I have to select a new teacher, I rely on my women's intuition, and it almost always works" (Robin, with three years of experience as an elementary school principal).

Relying on unconscious intuition—independent of reasoning, perception, or proof—may reflect principals' perception of teaching ability as an intangible spark that would attract kids or qualify a candidate as a worthy teacher.

Notably, quite a few of the interviewed principals expressed the belief that the desired characteristics of teachers will depend on the specific educational context. With regard to significant school characteristics, for instance, Kenneth, with 14 years of experience as a junior high school principal, claimed that rural areas need different teachers: "I believe that schools in the countryside are substantially different. While residents of metropolitan areas are competitive and look mainly for results, our parents have other priorities. Therefore, we need different teachers." (see Chapter 7 and 8 above).

More broadly, Susan, with 22 years of experience as an elementary school principal, stated: "There is no one model of the teacher I want for my school. It depends on the specific class, the school's needs at that time, the qualities of the teachers I have already, and so on." For Susan, the characteristics of desired teachers are not absolutes but rather vary according to circumstances at the time of the hiring process.

In sum, for principals, there is no simple answer to the question of which candidates are most suitable to work as a teacher in their schools and how principals can identify them. Principals do ascribe importance to teacher selection. However, in present-day schools, principals seem to undertake screening and hiring processes without sufficient evidence-based knowledge about such procedures' effectiveness. They contend that the task is too complex and that the desired qualifications are too indefinable to quantify or prioritize, changing according to the particular context. Thus, the hiring process for teachers today often relies more on intuition than reasoning.

The Unpleasantness of Teacher Dismissal

My recent research analysis of diverse principals' voices and perceptions (Shaked, 2019), undertaken to explore why principals tend to avoid human-resources management areas of their leadership role, highlighted a second major area of complexity involved in ensuring teachers' job suitability: the tension and disagreeable climate surrounding any decision to dismiss a teacher. Principals clarified that they did attribute high importance to the removal of ineffective teachers, but they reported that they often refrained from firing even those teachers who were consistently ineffective.

These interviewed school principals pointed to two major difficulties related to teachers' dismissal: existing teacher tenure policies, which restrict principals' ability to fire teachers, and the interpersonal aspect. These two non-instructional considerations led principals to avoid engaging in the firing of unsuitable teachers, as might be expected of them as part of their priorities as instructional leaders.

First, with regard to the policy-related barriers, principals often claimed that teacher dismissal is actually impractical because of national unionized teacher tenure policies:

- "Tenure makes removal of poorly performing teachers, who have actually been proven to be ineffective in the classroom, simply impossible" (Olga, with 11 years of experience as an elementary school principal).
- "Building a case for dismissal is time-consuming and draining for principals, and, after all that, the lousy teacher ends up remaining in the job" (Timothy, with nine years of experience as an elementary school principal).
- "Firing substandard teachers could be very useful. However, the Teachers Union is perhaps the most powerful lobbying group, so I don't even try" (Angela, with nine years of experience as an elementary school principal).

Second, with regard to the interpersonal barriers, many principals expressed the perception that teacher dismissal is one of the principal's most difficult and painful tasks and that it never gets easier. For example, Lisa, with five years of experience as a junior high school principal, described herself as unable to harm a teacher's livelihood: "No school wants bad teachers, but a teacher is also a human being, who needs to be a breadwinner. So, I will try to improve weak teachers' practices, but I won't make any teacher destitute. It's really a matter of human lives." Lisa eschewed teacher dismissal because of its potential economic damage to teachers. However, by retaining poorly performing teachers, Lisa agreed to lower her school's teaching quality.

A sentiment often voiced by these principals was the difficulty in firing a poorly functioning teacher due to the warm, long-term relationships among school staff members. For example, Pamela, with four years of experience as a principal in the same elementary school where she had previously worked as a teacher for decades, admitted with candor that after so many years of working together, she could not fire an ineffective teacher: "The fact is that she doesn't know how to teach. She is really unprofessional. But since we grew alongside each other and took part in each other's celebrations and losses, I simply cannot tell her to go home." Despite the instructional imperative, Pamela veered away from her role because of the discomfort involved in firing a longtime workmate. (Note that the mutual influences of interpersonal relationships and instructional leadership are discussed in almost every chapter of this book.)

Some principals explained how teacher tenure and the interpersonal aspect are often connected. For example, with 17 years of experience as an elementary school principal, Shirley claimed that "the long process required to remove a tenured teacher makes teacher dismissal counterproductive" because of its negative influence on the interpersonal relationships among staff.

Viewing the entire school team as a whole, Shirley believed that her school could tolerate a few weak teachers and thus preferred to dodge a demoralizing conflict-ridden atmosphere among school staff that might ensue if she undertook a dismissal process. Shirley seemed to believe that such a negative and resentful "murky" teacher climate could lead to broader deterioration in teaching quality, which would end up resembling the current local situation caused by the few poorly performing teachers.

Several principals rejected the need for teacher dismissal altogether. David, with six years of experience as a high school principal, said: "Teachers are comfortable coming to me for help. I have never come across a teacher who cannot improve his practices with the proper help."

Similarly, with seven years of experience as an elementary school principal, Robert claimed that a principal should focus on the bright side of leadership: "I believe that my main means of influence is through positive relationships and positive development of teachers. I seek to increase teachers' intrinsic motivation, appealing to their ideals." Through this lens, he objected to teacher dismissal: "Getting rid of the relatively weaker teachers, which is for me an act of aggression or even violence, does not solve any problem." Thus, unlike other principals, David and Robert did not explain their opposition to teacher dismissal in terms of teacher tenure or the possible negative consequences. Rather, they emphasized a perception of effective school leadership as concentrating on positive influences rather than adverse actions such as dismissal.

In sum, the firing of ineffective in-service teachers was perceived by principals as a potential action characterized by low chances of success and multiple drawbacks. Considering dismissal's difficulty and accompanying disadvantages, principals reported that, by and large, they most often preferred to retain unsuitable teachers whose instructional quality was not up to par, thus disregarding instructional leadership considerations.

CONCLUSION

My study (Shaked, 2019) sought to better understand why the human-resources management task of ensuring prospective and in-service teachers' job suitability was notably absent from conceptual frameworks for principals' instructional leadership. This study's outcomes highlighted the ambivalence and unease with which principals regarded their personnel management activities, such as deciding which attributes are most important for effective teachers, determining how to screen such effective teachers proficiently, and executing dismissal of ineffective teachers in order to improve the school. Apparently, such uncertainty and apprehension led principals to reject or circumvent those human-resources tasks by avoiding them, by regarding them as impossible or impractical, or by intuiting them via gut instinct instead of methodically as they would handle other instruction-related leadership tasks.

Principals apparently perceive the hiring and firing role as too complicated to address effectively; therefore, they do not consider it to be a means available to them to utilize in their day-to-day efforts to improve teaching and learning in the school. Whereas principals view tasks such as encouraging teachers to develop professionally, conducting observations in classrooms on a regular basis, and meeting individually with teachers to discuss student progress as "doable" tasks that can improve instruction and directly affect student achievement, the task of ensuring the fundamental job suitability of teachers is seen as "hard to do," with limited chances of success. Thus, actions related to selecting effective teachers to hire and dismissing ineffective teachers are not perceived as part of the instructional leadership toolbox.

PRACTICAL RECOMMENDATIONS ON ENSURING TEACHERS' JOB SUITABILITY FOR POLICYMAKERS, PRINCIPAL EDUCATORS, SUPERINTENDENTS, AND PRINCIPALS

- Principals should become aware that hiring good teachers and firing poor teachers will significantly impact their promotion of learning and achievement in school; hence, they should see this as a critical component of their instructional leadership responsibility.
- Principals should understand that the process of selecting a new teacher needs to be structured, systematic, and data based.
- Principals should acquire up-to-date knowledge on research that has pinpointed the major attributes, behaviors, and dispositions of effective teachers.
- Principals should be provided with practical methods enabling them to identify the desired characteristics in teacher applicants; in particular, principal educators and superintendents should assist principals in acquiring these skills.
- Principals should learn how to assess the suitability of a candidate teacher in terms of person-job fit, person-organization fit, and person-group fit within their particular school context.
- Principals should be given more leeway for personnel management, including flexibility in employing and dismissing tenured teachers; thus, policymakers should reexamine legislation and superintendents should provide practical support for principals in finding creative solutions for tenure policies.
- Principals should recognize the negative consequences of retaining chronically ineffective teachers when motivated solely by the desire to avoid damaging teacher-principal relationships. Principals' mentors should provide them with concrete tools for handling teachers' emotional reactions and conflictual working climate that may arise when facing a colleague's dismissal.

REFERENCES

Atteberry, A., Loeb, S., & Wyckoff, J. (2013). *Do first impressions matter? Improvement in early career teacher effectiveness.* American Institutes for Research.

Connell, R. (2009). Good teachers on dangerous ground: Towards a new view of teacher quality and professionalism. *Critical Studies in Education, 50*(3), 213–229.

Darling-Hammond, L. (2006). *Powerful teacher education: Lessons from exemplary programs.* Jossey-Bass.

Darling-Hammond, L., & Baratz-Snowden, J. (2005). *A good teacher in every classroom: Preparing the highly qualified teachers our children deserve*. Jossey-Bass.

Hallinger, P., & Murphy, J. (1985). Assessing the instructional management behavior of principals. *The Elementary School Journal, 86*(2), 217–247.

Harris, D., Rutledge, S., Ingle, W., & Thompson, C. (2010). Mix and match: What principals really look for when hiring teachers. *Education Finance and Policy, 5*(2), 228–246.

Harrison, J., Smithey, G., McAffee, H., & Weiner, C. (2006). Assessing candidate disposition for admission into teacher education: Can just anyone teach? *Action in Teacher Education, 27*(4), 72–80.

Ingle, K., Rutledge, S., & Bishop, J. (2011). Context matters: Principals' sensemaking of teacher hiring and on-the-job performance. *Journal of Educational Administration, 49*(5), 579–610.

Jacob, B. A. (2011). Do principals fire the worst teachers? *Educational Evaluation and Policy Analysis, 33*(4), 403–434.

Liu, L. (2009). Personal knowledge in educational autobiography: An investigation on "good teachers." *Frontiers of Education in China, 4*(1), 123–132.

Maddison, B. (2008). Labour commodification and classification: An illustrative case study of the New South Wales boilermaking trades, 1860–1920. *International Review of Social History, 53*(2), 235–260.

Malikow, M. (2006). Are teachers born or made? The necessity of teacher training programs. *National Forum of Teacher Education Journal, 16*(3), 1–3.

McChesney, R. W. (2011). Introduction. In N. Chomsky (Author), *Profit over people: Neoliberalism and global order* (pp. 7–16). Seven Stories.

Mezzadri, A. (2016). Class, gender and the sweatshop: On the nexus between labour commodification and exploitation. *Third World Quarterly, 37*(10), 1877–1900.

Nixon, A., Packard, A., & Dam, M. (2016). Teacher contract non-renewal: What matters to principals? *International Journal of Educational Leadership Preparation, 11*(1).

Range, B. G., Duncan, H. E., Scherz, S. D., & Haines, C. A. (2012). School leaders' perceptions about incompetent teachers: Implications for supervision and evaluation. *Bulletin of the National Association of Secondary School Principals, 96*(4), 302–322.

Robinson, V. (2007). *School leadership and student outcomes: Identifying what works and why*. Australian Council for Educational Leaders.

Scott, C., & Dinham, S. (2008). Born not made: The nativist myth and teachers' thinking. *Teacher Development, 12*(2), 115–124.

Shaked, H. (2019). Ensuring teachers' job suitability: A missing component of instructional leadership. *Journal of School Leadership, 29*(5), 427–447.

Stronge, J. H., Richard, H. B., & Catano, N. (2008). *Qualities of effective principals*. Association for Supervision and Curriculum Development.

Wiens, P. D., & Ruday, S. (2014). Personality and preservice teachers: Does it change, does it matter? *Issues in Teacher Education, 22*(2), 7–27.

Winters, M. A. (2012). *Transforming tenure: Using value-added modeling to identify ineffective teachers (Civic Report No. 70)*. Center for State and Local Leadership.

Chapter 10

Assistant Principals' Incomplete Application of Instructional Leadership

ABSTRACT

Both head principals and assistant principals face demands to apply instructional leadership. However, the literature on instructional leadership application has focused mainly on head principals while relatively neglecting assistant principals' instructional leadership application. The current chapter presents those particular domains of instructional leadership that assistant principals generally tend to avoid—those involving strategic leadership, authority, and personnel management. In light of the specific characteristics of the assistant principal's educational work, this chapter asserts the need for a targeted framework that specifically defines the instructional responsibilities of assistant principals, possibly while excluding instructional practices that involve the three avoided areas. Finally, the chapter points to practical recommendations about assistant principals' application of instructional leadership.

THE ASSISTANT PRINCIPAL AS NUMBER TWO IN THE SCHOOL HIERARCHY

Traditionally, assistant principals have been heavily involved in schools' day-to-day operations. These individuals might be the ones who arrange a replacement for an absent teacher, keep order in the cafeteria, and deal with discipline problems. However, as schools face an era of greater accountability for student achievement, assistant principals' role in monitoring teachers' efforts to raise academic results has become more imperative.

Inasmuch as standardized testing continues to assume a prominent place in education systems, the principal is no longer capable of facing the growing requirements and expectations for school effectiveness alone; the assistant principal must help in meeting the constant demand for improving student achievements. However, only a few studies have directly explored instructional leadership application in assistant principals, prompting Cranston and colleagues (2004, p. 225) to refer to them as "forgotten leaders."

From the school's micro-politics perspective (Ball, 2014), the positioning of assistant principals as number two in the hierarchal system holds intrinsic complexity because it is devoid of the status that the position of head principal entails. In comparison with the school's head principal, the assistant principal has much less access to sources of influence. Coercion, reward, and legitimate powers are reserved to the principal.

Assistant principals are expected to provide support—both personal and professional—to the principal, while also standing at the front lines to face various challenges. Although assistant principals are members of the principal's inner circle and active parties to school decision-making processes, they are constrained by the political dynamics of their school structure, which leaves them as marginalized leaders.

Thus, the position of the assistant principal in the organizational hierarchy is inherently conflictual. This fundamental ambiguity in the role of assistant principals invites different interpretations and expectations on the side of the principal, the professional and managerial staff, the community, the parents, and the students.

My recent empirical study focused on how assistant principals may or may not apply different aspects of the instructional leadership approach (Shaked, 2020). The research findings revealed that assistant principals perceived themselves as consistently refraining from three types of instructional leadership activities: those involving strategic leadership, those involving authority, and those involving personnel management.

Importantly, the assistant principals' avoidance of these three activity areas was by agreement with their principals. Assistant principals did not express a sense that their head principals were not allowing them access to those roles, and at the same time they did not describe themselves as refusing to perform tasks expected of them by their principals. Despite the importance of instructional leadership to school performance and student achievement, and although the principal alone cannot fulfill all the functions of instructional leadership, assistant principals were not interested in engaging in these activities, and their principals agreed to this. These three types of avoided instructional leadership activities are presented next.

Avoidance of Activities Involving Strategic Leadership

Assistant principals reported that they did not engage in instructional leadership activities that they deemed were under the purview of strategic leadership. They left those activities, which required taking responsibility for the "big picture," to their principals.

One such instructional leadership area related to strategic leadership that assistant principals did not undertake was the establishment of the school's instructional mission. When it came to setting the school's instructional purpose and goals, assistant principals perceived themselves as not standing at the forefront. They saw the principal as in complete charge of the process of setting school goals, while they saw themselves mostly as advisers.

For example, Justin, with three years of experience as an assistant elementary school principal, said: "The principal, not me, is responsible for establishing a vision of commitment to high standards and the success of all students. I'm definitely in a fairly senior position at school, but I'm number two rather than number one."

Similarly, Ronald, with 12 years of experience as an assistant junior high school principal, commented: "The principal leads our staff collaboratively to build the school's vision around student achievement. This is her job, not mine."

Inasmuch as the creation of the school vision was seen as beyond the assistant principal's range of responsibility, in schools where their principal did not prioritize instructional improvement, assistant principals felt limited in their ability to render change in this area. Peggy, with 19 years of experience as an assistant elementary school principal, described herself as believing deeply in the importance of improving instruction but felt largely constrained in her ability to contribute to her school's teaching and learning because of her principal's lack of focus on this goal: "It's impossible to significantly advance school processes that the principal doesn't fully believe in. It's clear to me that pedagogy is the most significant thing, but as long as my principal is not entirely with me, I can't really promote it."

In particular, assistant principals considered the principal as solely responsible for the strategic connections between the extra-school world and the school's instructional mission. This external world included the school board as the immediate formal authority and employer of both the principal and school staff; the parents, either as individuals or as an organized actor in the form of a parents' committee; policymakers at the national and regional levels; and the local community.

Assistant principals considered it the principal's "business" to work with all these stakeholders as partners for creating an instructional vision and to communicate the existing vision to them. Connie, with four years of experience as an assistant elementary school principal, explained: "I believe I will be a school principal one day, and probably it will be pretty soon, but for now everything that is related to external relations—only the principal deals with that."

Unlike some other assistant principals, who said they were not interested in becoming principals, Connie viewed her role as a stepping-stone to becoming principal. However, as long as she remained assistant principal, Connie planned on leaving the relations with the extra-school world to her head principal.

Another aspect of strategic leadership that assistant principals reported frequently leaving to their principals was the task of leading instructional discussions. Assistant principals seldom led meetings and discussions, even when those meetings pertained directly to instructional issues for which they were responsible.

Pauline, with nine years of experience as an assistant junior high school principal, explained: "I do a lot of one-on-one pedagogical work. But when it comes to meetings, it's his [the principal's] job to run them. . . . He does it well, but it's not just that. It's just something I don't do."

Avoidance of Activities Involving Authority

Assistant principals indicated that activities involving activation of authority were another instructional leadership area that they often left to their principals. They expressed the belief that the principal is the one person in the school who has both the right and the "clout" to tell people what to do and what not to do.

Thus, one of the most prominent examples given by assistant principals in relation to authority concerned the establishment of instructional guidelines. When it was necessary to set up instructional guidelines for staff, assistant principals often asked their principal to issue those guidelines. These guidelines dealt with areas such as "using a range of teaching methods and materials for inclusive teaching" (Jeanne, with seven years of experience as an assistant junior high school principal) or "ensuring that there is alignment between learning outcomes and teaching methods" (Debbie, with 10 years of experience as an assistant elementary school principal).

Assistant principals mentioned several motivations for seeking the principals' authoritative position when transmitting rules or policies to the school staff. For example, Anita, with 16 years of experience as an assistant elementary school principal, asserted that teachers responded with more deference to guidelines when issued by the principal than when issued by the assistant principal: "I have an excellent status at school, and I am very authoritative toward the teachers; however, as soon as the principal publishes instructions, they are treated differently."

Sherry, with four years of experience as an assistant elementary school principal, emphasized the formality of the principal's authority: "It's not a matter of whether they follow my instructions or not. These pieces [guidelines] govern the day-to-day occurrences that happen in our buildings, so they must be issued by the most senior person in the school."

Similarly, Amber, with five years of experience as an assistant elementary school principal, believed that in regard to instructional policies there is no room for collaborative leadership: "I know that today we talk about 'distributed' leadership [gesturing quotation marks in the air with her fingers]. However, school policies and procedures are the essential parts of any school, and so must be issued by the principal." From this perspective, as the most authoritative figure in the school, the head principal was seen by the assistant principals as needing to lead from the top rather than from the center.

Assistant principals noted that even when they themselves had initiated instructional guidelines, they preferred the guidelines to be disseminated formally through the principal's office. Pam, with nine years of experience as an assistant junior high school principal, explained the process: "The pedagogical guidelines that our principal sends to teachers are usually things I tell her to send. But I want them to come from her."

Likewise, Juan, with eight years of experience as an assistant elementary school principal, claimed that he was the one who wrote the pedagogical instructions, and the principal only sent them: "In actual fact, the person who really promotes teaching and learning in our school is me. The role of the principal is only to make sure that people follow our pedagogical policy."

An additional area that assistant principals left in the hands of principals was the handling of "defiant" teachers who resisted the assistant principals' instructional guidelines. Assistant principals considered themselves as persons viewed by teachers with respect and as holding authority over teachers. They were not afraid to tell teachers what to do and even to scold them when they did not perform their jobs properly. However, when a teacher consistently failed to follow their pedagogical instructions, assistant principals often involved the principal.

Erica, with 10 years of experience as an assistant elementary school principal, described a veteran teacher whose fixed beliefs about teaching led her to resist new teaching methods aiming to improve student outcomes: "She didn't agree to implement a pedagogical program that I led, claiming that we were wasting money on something that would be replaced in few years." When the teacher continued to resist despite Erica's attempts to reason with her, Erica asked the principal to talk to her: "Obviously, it's much harder for teachers to say no to the principal. Hard cases I always transfer to his treatment. He's the manager, so he'll find a way to handle it." It is interesting to note this discrepancy between how assistant principals referred to their principals' authority as opposed to the way in which the principals themselves reported their lack of power (see Chapter 6).

Similarly, assistant principals often asked their principals for approval of their instructional decisions, as shown in the following excerpts: "I am responsible for the professional development of the teachers, but before I finally decide on a course, I make sure my principal thinks like me" (Grace, with seven years of experience as an assistant elementary school principal); "I do not decide on my textbooks alone, though I can. I want the principal to be my partner in the decision making" (Jeffrey, with 11 years of experience as an assistant elementary school principal); "I decided which students would receive scholastic help, but in any cases of doubt I involved the principal" (Ruby, with three years of experience as an assistant junior high school principal). These examples illustrate how assistant principals seek out their principal's approval for every significant decision rather than feeling free to make some decisions—at least those that are not very significant—alone.

Avoidance of Activities Involving Personnel Management

Another instructional leadership area that assistant principals usually did not handle was management of human resources. They expressed a clear belief that a school's instructional leader should make sure that only those who are able to provide good teaching become part of the school staff (see Chapter 9). However, they said that although they were involved in teacher selection and hiring, the principal clearly managed this area.

Some assistant principals participated in screening résumés, interviewing, or observing candidates' demonstration lessons. Yet, the final hiring authority was always the principal's. Marion, with two years of experience as an assistant elementary school principal, clarified: "Hiring isn't something our principal does solo. She invites mid-level leaders to participate in this process. However, it will be her culpability if the person turns out to be deficient, so the final decision is always hers. We're just advisers."

Assistant principals reported that they were sometimes involved in in-service teachers' periodic performance evaluations or decisions about teachers' tenure because the principal delegated some of his/her own evaluation responsibilities to them, but in these, too, final authority rested solely with the principal. To decide whether to grant tenure to a novice teacher, principals are expected to conduct classroom observations and to use their impressions from these observations as evidence for rating the teacher's performance.

Assistant principals stated that they sometimes helped their principal in observing lessons taught by probationary teachers and then reporting their impressions to the principal. However, the decision remained the responsibility of the principal alone, who would complete the formal written evaluations and resolve tenure status.

One evaluation task that assistant principals clearly left to their principals was evaluating in-service teachers who were candidates for promotion to higher salary ranks (see Chapter 8 above for more on teacher evaluation). Debra, with 21 years of experience as an assistant elementary school principal, explained: "Teacher evaluation is a very sensitive issue, which can cause real damage to interpersonal relations. The principal has no choice but to deal with it, but as long as I am not a principal, I ask my principal not to be involved in it."

Hazel, with four years of experience as an assistant elementary school principal, justified why she was not in a position to carry out such evaluations despite her administrative role in the school: "I'm a teacher and she's a teacher, so how can I evaluate her? The principal is above all of us, but I'm actually a teacher just like her." This excerpt reflects many assistant principals' view of themselves as equal to other teachers on staff, without considering their administrative role as granting them higher status than their teacher peers.

From this perspective, there is a fundamental difference between the principal and the assistant principal. The principal is one level above everyone else, while the rest are at the same level, including the assistant principal, who continues working in a teaching capacity while integrating administrative tasks.

The dismissal of ineffective teachers is actually difficult to perform because of teacher tenure policy. Therefore, this potential instructional leadership strategy does not occur often in schools (see Chapters 8 and 9 for more on this complexity in firing tenured teachers). However, the interviewed assistant principals who did mention the process of dismissing a teacher as having been carried out in their schools clarified that the principal alone dealt with the firing, not the assistant principal.

Stephanie, with 11 years of experience as an assistant elementary school principal, explained: "Firing a teacher is something so unpleasant that I beg my principal not to involve me in it. That's why there's a principal, so he'll do these difficult things." Assistant principals reported that they advised the principal regarding dismissals and served as the principal's confidante but did not consider themselves part of such decisions.

CONCLUSION

The findings of my study (Shaked, 2020), uncovering the voices of the sometimes "forgotten" assistant principals, suggest that their positioning as number two in the school's hierarchal system seriously limits the scope of their instructional leadership application. Accordingly, their reported practices do not include vital activities that were identified by research as characterizing effective instructional leaders (see Introduction and Table 1 above).

In particular, assistant principals reported avoiding central instructional leadership behaviors such as leading the organization as a whole, exercising authority, conducting relationships with the world outside school, or managing personnel. These roles are left to the principal, who remains the ultimate leader of the school.

As such, assistant principals described a pattern of behavior corroborating prior research that pinpointed assistant principals' much lower access to sources of power and influence than their principals (see Chapter 6 regarding low power distance), as well as the marginalizing constraints imposed by the political dynamics of their school structure (Bukoski et al., 2016; Leaf & Odhiambo, 2017; Norton, 2015). Thus, the instructional leadership of assistant principals may be seen as instructional sub-leadership, which lacks the power, status, and authority afforded by the principal position.

In the current era of accountability, head principals expect assistant principals to help them in monitoring teachers in order to improve student outcomes. Inasmuch as the principal cannot face the growing requirements for school performance alone, the assistant principal must help in meeting the exigent demands for high achievement. However, the findings of my recent study suggest that the influence of the assistant principal has not sufficiently evolved over recent years.

Unlike the principal, assistant principals do not perceive themselves as possessing ample formal or informal authority in the eyes of the school team. Assistant principals' insufficient micro-political power among teachers appears to limit the scope of their instructional leadership application.

PRACTICAL RECOMMENDATIONS ON ASSISTANT PRINCIPALS' INSTRUCTIONAL LEADERSHIP APPLICATION FOR POLICYMAKERS, PRINCIPAL EDUCATORS, SUPERINTENDENTS, PRINCIPALS, AND ASSISTANT PRINCIPALS

- Principals should be encouraged to expand the assistant principal's instructional leadership application. Simultaneously, assistant principals should be encouraged to take on the mantle of extended instructional leadership.
- Assistant principals should participate in strategic instructional leadership, becoming principals' partners in defining instructional goals, communicating with external stakeholders, and leading instructional discussions.
- Assistant principals should be considered (both formally and informally) as authority figures in the school, who can make decisions and set policies. Policymakers can play an important role in this matter.
- Assistant principals should be involved in human-resources management, including selecting new teachers, evaluating in-service teachers, and firing poor teachers.

REFERENCES

Ball, S. J. (2014). *The micro-politics of the school: Towards a theory of school organization*. Routledge.

Bukoski, B. E., Lewis, T. C., Carpenter, B. W., Berry, M. S., & Sanders, K. S. (2016). The complexities of realizing community: Assistant principals as community leaders in persistently low-achieving schools. *Leadership and Policy in Schools, 14*(4), 411–436.

Cranston, N., Tromans, C., & Reugebrink, M. (2004). Forgotten leaders: What do we know about the deputy principalship in secondary schools? *International Journal of Leadership in Education, 7,* 225–242.

Leaf, A., & Odhiambo, G. (2017). The deputy principal instructional leadership role and professional learning: Perceptions of secondary principals, deputies and teachers. *Journal of Educational Administration, 55*(1), 33–48.

Norton, M. S. (2015). *The assistant principal's guide: New strategies for new responsibilities*. Routledge.

Shaked, H. (2020). Boundaries of Israeli assistant principals' instructional leadership. *Leadership and Policy in Schools, 19*(3), 497–511.

PART IV

Paradoxical Solutions to Instructional Leadership Application

This part of the book offers some tools for instructional leaders in the form of the paradoxical approach, which advocates a "both/and" way of dealing with conflicting demands. Chapter 11 explains how to handle factors that inhibit instructional leadership application through the paradoxical approach. Chapter 12 then illustrates the paradoxical approach by examining the overlap between instructional leadership and boundary management, which seeks to regulate the boundary separating the school from its environment. This chapter proposes a new domain of school leadership—instructional boundary management—which is a synthesis of the two different complementary frameworks.

Chapter 11

A Paradoxical Approach to Instructional Leadership Application

ABSTRACT

This chapter shows how the paradoxical approach, which advocates a "both/and" orientation to conflicting demands, may moderate the influence of principals' inhibitory perceptions about instructional leadership, discussed in Chapter 4. The paradoxical approach allows school principals to hold conflicting perspectives on instructional leadership simultaneously. Thus, this approach reduces the effect of perceptions that inhibit instructional leadership application by permitting principals to delay their decisions about whether to fulfill the role of instructional leader or to disagree with it. The chapter ends with practical recommendations regarding utilization of the paradoxical approach to promote application of instructional leadership.

EMPLOYING A PARADOXICAL APPROACH TO OVERCOME THE PERCEPTIONS INHIBITING INSTRUCTIONAL LEADERSHIP

Organizations, as complex systems, are rife with conflicts and contradictions. Many of these contradictions may be seen as "either/or" challenges, where leaders evaluate the advantages and disadvantages of different options and then make tough decisions about them. In contrast, leaders who mobilize paradoxical behaviors have access to a "both/and" approach, which supports contradictory elements simultaneously by leveraging the advantages of each option separately and building on their synergistic potential. My recent research study (Shaked, 2020) explored how school principals' paradoxical approach may help lessen the influence of the inhibitory perceptions of instructional leadership application (see Chapter 4) and the tendency toward incomplete application of instructional leadership (see Part III) during school leaders' decision making.

Smith and Lewis (2012, p. 386) defined paradox as "contradictory yet interrelated elements that exist simultaneously and persist over time. Such elements seem logical when considered in isolation but irrational, inconsistent, and even absurd when juxtaposed." The paradoxical approach is grounded in the premise that these tensions represent opportunities for, rather than threats to, organizational growth and prosperity.

In non-paradoxical leadership, the leaders strive to resolve tensions within the organization in ways such as the "tradeoff," where leaders choose between alternatives that each have pros and cons, or the "compromise," which is based on concessions on all sides. Instead, paradoxical leaders "foster a deep appreciation and respect for paradoxical tensions" (Lewis et al., 2014, p. 63), valuing the positive energy enabled by paradox.

Through a paradoxical approach, leaders provide a guiding direction while emphasizing the need to address, adjust to, and excel at managing tensions. This approach helps individuals, groups, and organizations to be flexible and resilient in the face of real-world complexity and stress. Moreover, it fosters more dynamic decision making and creative solutions to problems.

Thus, paradoxical leaders seek to proactively raise tensions to the surface as an integral part of decision-making processes. Importantly, the paradoxical approach in people management has been associated with increased proficiency, adaptivity, and proactivity among employees, enabling the long-term sustainment of effectiveness (Lewis et al., 2014).

The extent to which leaders engage in the paradoxical approach was found to be positively related to their systems thinking (Zhang et al., 2015), which was described above (Chapter 3) as an enabler of instructional leadership application. When it comes to school principals, the paradoxical approach may be seen as reflecting *adopting a multidimensional view*, which is one of the characteristics of systems thinking in school leadership. *Adopting a multidimensional view* involves contemplation of several aspects of a given issue simultaneously.

In the eyes of holistic principals who perform at the systems level, each element or part within the vast and complex school system as a whole is regarded as having a context that influences it; therefore, there is always more than one reason, explanation, implication, or answer related to that part or element of interest (Shaked & Schechter, 2014, 2017). This perspective may lead to an ability to hold inconsistencies in mind simultaneously and to utilize a paradoxical approach.

My recent research (Shaked, 2020) revealed that the paradoxical approach does indeed enable many school principals to simultaneously hold conflicting perspectives regarding instructional leadership. Therefore, the paradoxical approach can moderate the effects of inhibitory perceptions of instructional leadership application while making room for principals to give greater weight to enabling factors.

This approach allows principals who do not fully agree with the need for instructional leadership and its effects to put aside the decision of whether to choose instructional leadership behavior at a given time. They can leave for later their choice between fulfilling the expectation to demonstrate instructional leadership on the one hand and their disagreements with it on the other hand.

Instead of focusing on the conflicts inherent in their leadership work or forcing themselves to choose one option over another, the paradoxical approach enables them to maintain both options simultaneously. The following sections illustrate a paradoxical approach to each of the inhibitory perceptions of instructional leadership mentioned above in Chapter 4: roles, schooling's goals, and relationships.

The Paradox in Instructional Leaders' Other Managerial Responsibilities

To recall, the first inhibitory perception of instructional leadership application lies in principals' role beliefs. Specifically, instructional leadership application is inhibited by principals' view that they do not need to focus mainly on instructional issues but rather can concentrate on other areas, such as setting up the proper conditions for teachers in terms of logistic arrangements, budget, and discipline as well as being a bridge to the extra-school world.

The paradoxical approach enables principals to juggle conflicting commitments simultaneously, paying attention to both instructional and other responsibilities. For example, Rita, with six years of experience as a high school principal, did not prioritize any one of her tasks over another but instead regarded each of them as a top priority. Instead of ranking her duties as a principal in order of importance, which might have resulted in her low ranking of instructional leadership application, she considered many of her different roles to all equally qualify as "the most important thing I do as a school principal." Thus, by attributing equally strong emphasis to various components of her work, Rita expressed a paradoxical approach, which advocates a "both/and" proposition to conflicting demands. These excerpts from Rita's interview exemplify her "both/and" approach:

- About school safety: "Protecting the students from bullying, harassment, violence, and substance usage is the most meaningful element of my work."
- About relationships with external stakeholders: "While the entire staff is taking care of what is going on inside the school, I am the only contact person with all the outside parties. Therefore, this is a main component of my job."
- About improvement of student learning: "Broadening and deepening students' knowledge base across various subjects is our mission as a school, so my main mission as a principal is to ensure high-level student learning."

Nicole, with 14 years of experience as an elementary school principal, also revealed a paradoxical ability to perceive herself as performing in two contradictory ways simultaneously. On the one hand, slightly diminishing the importance of her direct involvement in issues of teaching and learning, Nicole argued that she did not have to monitor teacher work: "My teachers learned the profession and gained experience, so I trust them to do the job properly." On the other hand, she considered it imperative to know what was going on inside each class: "I have to correctly recognize the performance of each teacher" because "I don't want to make a mistake by not knowing what is happening in classrooms."

In this context, she mentioned a well-known Jewish story about a rabbi who, when asked to decide on a dispute between two of his followers, told each of them "You're right." The rabbi's wife, who listened to the conversation, asked how both could be right, and the rabbi answered, "You're also right." Using this story, Nicole showed that she was aware of her paradoxical approach, solving the apparent logical failure with humor.

The Paradox in Instructional Leaders' Non-Academic Goals for Schooling

The second inhibitory perception of instructional leadership application concerns principals' argument that they should not become too focused on instructional issues because the school's primary task is non-academic—to meet students' emotional needs, impart moral values, and support their social integration. Like Rita in the previous section, Joe, with 12 years of experience as a junior high school principal, rated several of his school's goals as equally the "most" important. He ascribed "primary" importance to the school's role in developing students' emotional well-being, including their sense of belonging and safety, happiness in the present, and optimism regarding the future. He also claimed that schools need "more than anything" to develop students morally and to promote their desired character traits such as responsibility, self-control, integrity, decency, and good manners. At the same time, paradoxically, Joe also placed the learning and achievement of the students as a top priority of the school: "The school's first and foremost goal is to teach students literacy, math, and science."

Likewise, Sheila, with nine years of experience as an elementary school principal, argued on the one hand that "the primary role of schools is to deliver classroom instruction that helps students learn." At the same time, she also asserted: "Prioritizing student achievement is based on a very narrow point of view, which considers schools as only preparing young people for higher education and employment. Developing their emotional well-being, including their sense of belonging and safety, is no less important." Neither Joe nor Sheila seemed to focus on the conflicts between their different school goals (i.e., on the "either/or" nature of their views), instead appearing to be at peace with their paradoxical "both/and" approach.

Likewise, Harold, with 11 years of experience as an elementary school principal, described himself as devoting a great deal of time to programs designed to give students the social tools required to function within their society, for example, teaching students to navigate social interactions with peers from different backgrounds and helping them become productive community members who work not only toward their own goals but also on behalf of the public. At the same time, he also depicted himself as paying attention to his school's academic and non-academic goals simultaneously. He said he was deeply involved in a wide range of instructional leadership activities, such as aligning curriculum, assessment, and instruction as well as using data to improve learning.

The Paradox in Instructional Leaders' Relationships with Teachers

The third of principals' perceptions that inhibit their instructional leadership application stems from their belief that close principal-teacher relationships are of utmost significance and may be undermined if principals consistently critique their teachers' practice. Several principals interviewed in this recent research study (Shaked, 2020) appeared to be capable of paradoxical behavior with regard to their relationships with teachers.

That is, some principals did develop close relationships with their teachers but at the same time regularly supervised their teachers' work, despite their knowledge that this supervision would make it difficult to maintain a positive tone in the relationships. Thus, instead of choosing to have close relationships with teachers by avoiding monitoring of teachers' work, these principals performed both simultaneously.

For example, Diana, with seven years of experience as an elementary school principal, described herself as investing a great deal in fostering her positive relationships with the teaching staff: "I don't forget to take an interest in the health of sick teachers and family events of teachers, both happy and unfortunate" and "I greet teachers every morning at the school entrance and sit in the teachers' room during the breaks."

However, she described herself as also monitoring teachers' practices: "The most effective way I have found to monitor teachers' work is to sit in on their classes. Then there must be a one-on-one conversation, pointing out strengths, areas where improvement is needed, and ways to improve." She was aware that "teachers hate to be observed when teaching," and therefore noted that "my observations and my criticism of teacher work do not make me a favorite of teachers."

Thus, from Diana's perspective, relationships between the principal and her teachers were essential, and so she nurtured them. At the same time, to produce student graduates with satisfactory academic results, she realized that processes designed to monitor teaching quality were needed. These two sets of actions were not fully compatible because close monitoring might spoil relationships. Nevertheless, Diana dealt with both issues simultaneously, demonstrating the paradoxical approach.

Similarly, Joshua, with 17 years of experience as an elementary school principal, described his relationship with teachers as characterized by "mutual trust and friendship among people who spend a lot of time together and have each other's back." However, he was a proponent of the principal's monitoring of students' learning progress: "If students' results are not systematically inspected, and teachers are not held accountable for their students' achievements, I would not expect real improvements."

Joshua understood that when he "inspects teachers repeatedly," he is not "creating a friendly place to work." The contradiction between describing the atmosphere as involving "mutual trust and friendship" but not a "friendly" workplace reflects the paradoxical approach.

CONCLUSION

As human beings, principals have an internal need for consistency. Naturally, they experience cognitive dissonance when faced with apparent contradictions, which triggers the desire to remove the discomfort. According to my study, however, school reality forces principals to embrace the paradoxical approach. When espousing this approach, principals feel more comfortable in situations with underlying tensions or conflicting demands. Instead of eliminating tensions, they learn to accept them, feel comfortable with them, and see them as opportunities.

Specifically, my study illustrated how the paradoxical approach may moderate the inhibiting influence of some of principals' major perceptions about instructional leadership application while giving the enablers of instructional leadership a chance to make a bigger impact. The keen relevance of the paradoxical approach stems from the fact that each of the three major inhibitory perceptions of instructional leadership application is based on tension between the principal's instructional leadership role and the principal's other duties, responsibilities, and priorities.

By facilitating a "both/and" approach to these tensions, principals were not required to make explicit choices between different options. Thus, the paradoxical approach allowed principals to prevent turning their opposition to instructional leadership application into sheer avoidance of its implementation.

PRACTICAL RECOMMENDATIONS ON THE PARADOXICAL APPROACH TO INSTRUCTIONAL LEADERSHIP APPLICATION FOR POLICYMAKERS, PRINCIPAL EDUCATORS, SUPERINTENDENTS, AND PRINCIPALS

- Principals should develop a paradoxical approach to principalship in general, and particularly to instructional leadership application, where they view conflicts and dilemmas as organizational growth opportunities.
- Principals should be provided with opportunities (for example, in advanced training) to learn to integrate supervision of teacher practices and student results with healthy principal-teacher relationships.
- Principals should understand how to juggle the variety of responsibilities they have, handling different duties together. They should learn and reflect on the integration and separation of duties.
- Principals should prioritize both academic and non-academic school goals, recognizing these goals' reciprocal ability to enrich each other.

REFERENCES

Lewis, M. W., Andriopoulos, C., & Smith, W. K. (2014). Paradoxical leadership to enable strategic agility. *California Management Review*, *56*(3), 58–77.

Shaked, H. (2020). A paradoxical approach to instructional leadership. *International Journal of Educational Management*, *34*(10), 1637–1646.

Shaked, H., & Schechter, C. (2014). Systems school leadership: Exploring an emerging construct. *Journal of Educational Administration, 52*(6), 792–811.

Shaked, H., & Schechter, C. (2017). *Systems thinking for school leaders: Holistic leadership for excellence in education.* Springer.

Smith, W. K., & Lewis, M. W. (2012). Leadership skills for managing paradoxes. *Industrial and Organizational Psychology, 5*(2), 227–231.

Zhang, Y., Waldman, D. A., Han, Y. L., & Li, X. B. (2015). Paradoxical leader behaviors in people management: Antecedents and consequences. *Academy of Management Journal, 58*(2), 538–566.

Chapter 12

A Paradoxical Approach in Practice

Instructional Leadership Application and Boundary Management

ABSTRACT

This last chapter illustrates how the paradoxical approach to instructional leadership application, discussed in the previous chapter, enables the merging of two different frameworks—instructional leadership and boundary management—with each other. Alongside the importance of instructional leadership application, one of the most persistent and potentially rewarding challenges facing principals is their boundary management, which includes both internal and external boundary activities. Based on the paradoxical approach, a new area of school leadership is suggested—instructional boundary management—which is a synthesis of the two frameworks. The chapter concludes with pragmatic recommendations regarding the paradoxical approach for practicing instructional leadership and boundary management.

PRINCIPALS' BOUNDARY ACTIVITIES

In recent years, new trends toward decentralization and bottom-up policy implementation at the school level have increased the individual school's decision-making authority. Greater autonomy at the local level has transformed schools into open systems upholding a close relationship with their resource-providing environment. They must walk a tight line between, on the one hand, the school's internal needs and capacities and, on the other hand, the external desires and demands that come from official sources (such as the district) and unofficial sources (such as the school community). The principals must facilitate and reach agreement among these various stakeholders. In order to be able to guide the school in responding to expectations and standards set by external agents, principals must assume the role of facilitating the transfer of assets and information both into and out of the school from/to its surroundings.

Research has shown that far from being self-contained isolated systems, schools are nested organizations having multiple connections that are employed to increase the school's interdependence with elements in its environment (Valli et al., 2018; Wang, 2018). These connections turn schools into open systems, which are embedded in an environment that may include parents, community members, school district personnel, government agencies, and other external stakeholders upon which the school relies for many of its instructional materials and resources.

Contemporary schools' boundaries are permeable and blurred, characterized by reciprocal influences between the schools and outside elements, as well as the establishment of new relational patterns. Inasmuch as schools cannot generate all necessary resources from within but rather depend on their environment for resources essential for their survival, principals must span the boundary and enable high levels of interactions with critical external parties. Thus, maintaining healthy relations with external constituencies in the school environment has become a pivotal role of principals.

Against this backdrop, principals are increasingly involved in "boundary management"—behaviors aiming to regulate the boundary that separates the school from its environment. In this regard, research has indicated that principals seek to ensure that the school boundary becomes neither too tightly delineated nor too permeable (Benoliel, 2017; Benoliel & Somech, 2018).

On the one hand, principals can maintain a tight boundary around the school, creating an environment that strengthens the feeling of belonging among the school's staff, protecting the school from information overload, and reducing external pressures. On the other hand, by keeping a loose boundary around the school, principals can promote the search for new information, mobilize support and legitimacy, and increase attentiveness to changes in the school's environment. Striving to balance the permeability of the school boundary, principals have to ascribe much attention to boundary management, which comprises a wide range of boundary-related activities.

Today's principals, who are constantly asked to demonstrate instructional leadership, run systems that are characterized by growing openness and therefore are often engaged in boundary activities. Thus, principals find themselves frequently juggling the two demanding roles of instructional leaders and boundary managers. The current chapter explores how the paradoxical approach allows instructional leadership and boundary management to function in reciprocal ways so as to complement one another or substitute for each other.

To gain a thorough understanding of school principals' boundary management activities, Benoliel (2017; Benoliel & Somech, 2018) explored Druskat and Wheeler's (2003) typology in the school context. Drawing upon Benoliel's research, principals' boundary activities are discussed next, with a focus first on internal and then on external issues relative to the school.

Internal Activities

Principals must focus on internal activities, which are those involving internal school matters occurring within the school boundary, including activities aimed at *relating, scouting, persuading,* and *empowering* (Benoliel, 2017). Such internal activities serve to distinguish the school from its environment because these activities enable the establishment of the school's own workspace, distinctiveness, and purposes, thereby refining the school boundary from within.

The internal *relating* activities involve such behaviors as building trust among faculty members and demonstrating fairness to school members in the decision-making process. The internal *scouting* activities involve searching for information about strengths, weaknesses, and difficult issues that faculty members face. This is accomplished by examining problems methodically. Principals initiate communication with school staff in an effort to acquire information about internal events, experiences, and needs in order to identify and clarify information that might be useful to the decision-making process.

The internal *persuading* activities involve convincing faculty to set priorities in line with school goals and to create a common vision. A common vision may be a source for creating a shared language, ultimately transforming the individual ideas of school members into shared school instructional processes and practices. A common vision gathers school staff for a combined effort, enhancing commitment to school goals and instructional processes. The internal *empowering* activities involve delegating authority, exercising flexibility regarding school staff decisions, and coaching.

External Activities

Principals must also focus on external activities, which likewise include *relating, scouting,* and *persuading* activities (Benoliel, 2017). Through external activities, the principal represents the school to external stakeholders to access and secure resources and support, and the principal monitors the external environment for information or events that could hinder or enhance the achievement of school goals.

The external *relating* activities involve building positive relationships between the school and out-of-school stakeholders, such as learning about external stakeholders' power structures and arrangements as well as maintaining positive connections with parents and the community. Principals constantly span the boundary by collaborating and cooperating with important communities outside of the school.

The external *scouting* activities involve searching for information from external stakeholders in order to identify important environmental events and then share this information with faculty members. Research indicates that strong partnerships with local institutions and mutually productive relationships with parents can help to provide important pedagogical and instructional resources. Acting as a filter and facilitator, principals' boundary spanning activities can protect the school core from information overload.

The principal's external *persuading* activities involve obtaining external support for the school. This means presenting the school to external stakeholders in a way that safeguards the interests of the school and maximizes the support available to the school.

In line with this distinction between internal and external boundary activities, in a recent study (Shaked & Benoliel, 2020), we found that principals were engaged in various behaviors that simultaneously reflected instructional leadership and boundary management. These principals' behaviors were divided into (1) those that reflected instructional leadership and internal boundary activities and (2) those that reflected instructional leadership and external boundary activities. These behaviors are presented in the next two sections.

Instructional Leadership and Internal Boundary Activities

The principals' behaviors that reflect instructional leadership as well as internal boundary activities include *internal instructional relating*, *internal instructional scouting*, *internal instructional persuading*, and *internal instructional empowering*, as described next.

Internal instructional relating refers to building trust among teachers to enable open discourse about strengths and weaknesses of instruction. Principals in our study (Shaked & Benoliel, 2020) perceived building trust, which is an internal boundary activity of *relating*, as a foundation for instructional leadership application.

For example, Regina, with nine years of experience as an elementary school principal, viewed trust as the foundation for effective supervision: "My supervision practices are not an evaluation directed toward giving a score. They are based on the goodwill of both sides to create opportunities for teachers to expand their capacity to teach effectively and to care for students." For Regina, the practice of professional supervision by school principals should involve supportive dialogue rather than judgment, thus requiring the principal to engender trust in the teacher in order to obtain honest disclosure of difficulties.

More broadly, Sally, with 14 years of experience as a high school principal, aspired to create trust not only between her, as principal, and the teachers under her supervision, but also among the teachers themselves. She considered such trust as essential for open discourse about strengths and weaknesses in the school's teaching climate: "I strive to create a safe climate, in which teachers feel free to invite feedback regarding their teaching and results and to share their perspectives in situations where there is a difference of opinion or conflict."

Internal instructional scouting refers to searching for information about the instructional difficulties and needs of teachers. Principals focused their attention on the instructional needs and difficulties of teachers. Meeting teachers' instructional needs and helping them solve their teaching problems clearly reflects the nucleus of instructional leadership, which requires principals to focus their efforts on improving teaching practices.

Methodically looking for teachers' needs, problems, strengths, and weaknesses also reflected the *scouting* internal boundary activity. The interviewed instructional leaders pointed to a wide range of instructional needs that they had identified among teachers, such as needs for autonomy, guidance, feedback, appreciation, available time, equipment, supplies, and working conditions.

These principals ascribed importance to, and even proactively sought to understand, the instructional needs prioritized by teachers, even when these were not their own priorities. Nicholas, with four years of experience as a high school principal, explained: "Principals have considerable control over the things that teachers desire most for their teaching, and many cost relatively little. It doesn't take a rocket scientist to understand what teachers want. You just have to ask and listen, that's all."

Florence, with 11 years of experience as a high school principal, expressed a similar point of view: "A principal who regularly engages with teachers and understands what they want for their teaching purpose is likely to be running a happy school whose teachers are very satisfied." Interestingly, principals were aware that different teachers have different needs, as stated by Mildred, with five years of experience as a high school principal: "Just like I expect teachers to know and understand their students as individuals and personalize their instruction according to the nuances of their learning, I must learn and meet my teachers' personalized needs related to their teaching."

Internal instructional persuading refers to convincing teachers to set priorities in line with school instructional goals and to create a common instructional vision. Principals disseminated the school's teaching and learning mission to teachers. Such behavior aiming to communicate the school's instructional goals to school staff reflects an important component of instructional leadership (see Introduction and Table 1).

At the same time, this behavior reflects *persuading* internal boundary activity. The dissemination activities mentioned by the interviewed principals were varied, involving aims such as broadening students' knowledge base in a small number of essential curricular domains like language and mathematics; achieving high results in external examinations; developing learning skills such as creative thinking and the ability to locate information; promoting students' love of learning; and cultivating enquiring minds. Importantly, principals noted multiple ways in which they deepened their teachers' connection to the school's vision of teaching and learning.

For example, Megan, with 14 years of experience as an elementary school principal, described herself as taking advantage of every opportunity to persuasively talk about her school's pedagogical vision: "I talk to teachers over and over again, on many occasions, about our pedagogical vision, to ensure that all teachers speak in one voice." Martin, with seven years of experience as a high school principal, emphasized that "Logic makes us think, emotion drives us to act. Emotion can come from analogies, stories, or concrete examples that illustrate to teachers what our success looks like."

Eric, with 12 years as a junior high school principal, said he was working with teacher leaders who could influence other teachers: "To generate common commitment to our scholastic goals, I identify key players within the teaching staff who will motivate other teachers to buy into the vision. I want central teachers to believe these goals and to pass them on to others."

Internal instructional empowering refers to entrusting responsibilities to teachers and exercising flexibility regarding teachers' instructional decisions. Principals mobilized leadership competence at all levels of the school in order to generate more opportunities for improving teaching, learning, and academic results.

Such activity reflects principals' reliance on the expertise of teacher leaders to improve school effectiveness, which is a main component of instructional leadership. In fact, it reflects "shared" instructional leadership (see Urick, 2016). At the same time, it reflects the internal boundary activity of *empowering* as detailed below. Principals described a wide range of responsibilities that they entrusted to mid-level teacher leaders, such as participating in the determination of instructional policies; guiding their teacher colleagues in how to implement effective teaching strategies; explaining to colleagues how to follow content standards; sharing instructional resources such as websites, textbooks, lesson plans, and assessment tools; and facilitating professional learning communities among staff members.

Most of the teacher-leaders mentioned by instructional leaders were formal mid-level position holders—teachers who held official management responsibility for a team of teachers or for an aspect of the school's work, such as grade-level heads, department heads, evaluation coordinators, instruction coordinators, and information and communications technology (ICT) coordinators. However, some others were informal leaders, whose roles emerged as teachers interacted with their peers, based on their talents and experience.

Instructional Leadership and External Boundary Activities

The principals' behaviors that reflect instructional leadership as well as external boundary activities include *external instructional relating*, *external instructional scouting*, and *external instructional persuading*, as described next.

External instructional relating refers to building positive relationships between the school and external stakeholders to mobilize support for instruction. Principals cultivated close relationships with the school board as the immediate formal authority and employer of both principal and school staff; the parents, either as individuals or in the form of a parents' committee as an organized actor; policymakers at the regional (and even the national) levels; and the local community. They perceived these healthy relationships as enabling other external activities—*instructional scouting* and *instructional persuading*.

External instructional scouting refers to searching for information about curriculum and instruction through formal and informal interactions with external actors. Principals' search for information from external actors in order to acquire knowledge that might be useful to improve teaching and learning clearly reflected an instructional leadership orientation. At the same time, it also reflected the *scouting* external boundary activity.

Principals were methodically looking for information about curriculum and instruction through both formal and informal interactions with external actors. Aaron, with nine years of experience as an elementary school principal, described himself as looking for instructional information in professional meetings: "I make sure to attend principal conferences, even though I have many of them, because that's where I keep up to date on standards, examinations, and new programs."

Annette, with five years of experience as a high school principal, also sought information about educational techniques in conferences, but mainly through informal interactions with other principals: "When I go to principals' meetings, what matters to me is not the meetings themselves, but the conversations with other principals, where I hear many important things about teaching methods, learning materials, etc."

Howard, with six years of experience as an elementary school principal, said he was "interested in what other schools do, to copy ideas and initiatives that might improve our achievements," and Denise, with 12 years of experience as a high school principal, said she maintained close relationships with district officials "so as not to miss out and to know first about new curriculums, exams, and guidelines."

External instructional persuading refers to obtaining external stakeholders' support for the school's instructional goals. Principals reported investing staunch efforts into obtaining such external support. As mentioned above in the introduction (see Table 1), communicating the school's instructional goals to various stakeholders is a main component of instructional leadership. At the same time, it reflects the *persuading* external boundary activity. While principals prioritized learning and achievements, some parents did not have the same opinion.

Wanda, with five years of experience as an elementary school principal, described: "What is most important to them [parents] is for their children to be happy." Those parents who prioritized non-academic over academic goals wanted reductions in homework, in the number of exams, and in the school workload. Wanda had had many conversations with them, trying to convince them regarding school priorities: "We need to help our 'customers' [gesturing quotation marks in the air with her fingers] understand that the happiness of their children cannot be achieved without learning at a high level." Viewing parents as the consumers of her school's services, Wanda did not describe collaborative thinking but rather attempts to persuasively explain to parents why the academic priorities of the school were the right ones.

Similarly, Cheryl, with eight years of experience as a high school principal, described parents who believed that the school's foremost goal should be to develop students morally and promote their desired character traits and good manners: "For me, face-to-face communication is ranked No. 1 for matching of expectations with parents. Raising young people of values is certainly important, but the main thing that happens in school is learning, and its importance cannot be underestimated."

While Wanda and Cheryl focused on the need to communicate their schools' instructional goals to parents, Larry, with 17 years of experience as a high school principal, reported that he had to convince local government officials of the importance of learning and academic outcomes: "The municipality wanted all schools to participate in a program that emphasized the non-academic, humanistic goals of education. I have spoken with them many times to convince them that we cannot neglect learning and achievement."

The Paradoxical Overlap Between Instructional Leadership and Boundary Management

One might claim that the frameworks of instructional leadership and boundary management focus their gaze on dissimilar aspects of principalship, which are separated both conceptually and functionally. From this point of view, instructional leadership application and engagement in boundary activities are two unconnected challenges faced by contemporary educational leaders.

However, the findings of our study (Shaked & Benoliel, 2020) show that through the paradoxical lens, these two frameworks have a significant area of overlap, specifying quite a few principalship behaviors that serve both as instructional leadership application and boundary management simultaneously. It seems that the management of instructional programs and school boundaries may somewhat merge with each other; thus, the conceptual distinction between them is blurred and should be softened.

The overlap of instructional leadership application and boundary management stems from the fact that instructional leadership application is not solely internal, and boundary management is not exclusively external. Instructional leaders focus not only on teaching, learning, and assessment activities taking place within the school but also on importing the resources, support, and knowledge from outside the school that are needed to improve academic results.

Principals explain the school's instructional mission to external stakeholders, create partnerships that help student learning, and search for information about teaching and curriculum outside the school's boundaries. At the same time, boundary management includes not only interactions with individuals, groups, and organizations outside the school but also many internal activities, which reinforce the school boundary from within. Caring for the school staff, strengthening teachers' sense of belonging, and protecting them from excessive external demands and a flood of information are essential components of boundary management.

Inasmuch as both instructional leadership application and boundary management comprise both internal and external activities, many behaviors associated with the principal's role reflect instructional leadership application and boundary management simultaneously. Moreover, instructional leadership application deals with the questions of *what* and *why*, while boundary management addresses the questions of *how* and *with whom*. Therefore, this

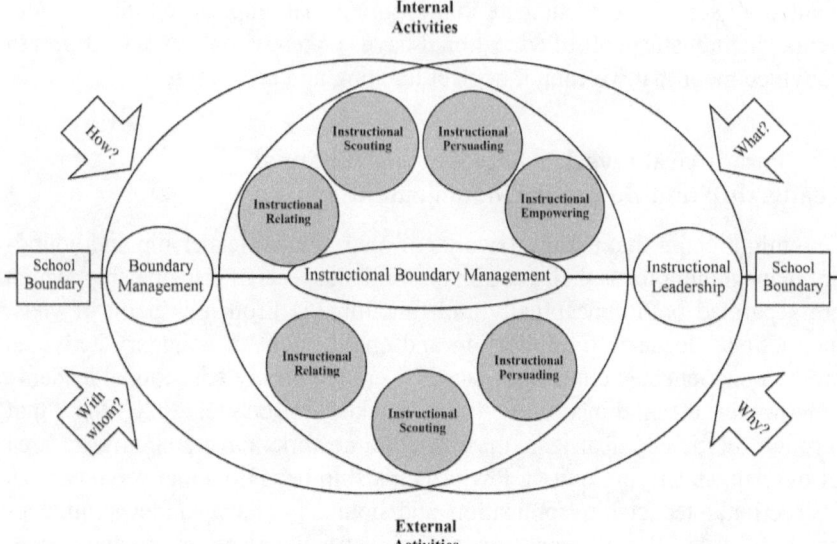

Figure 12.1. The Construct of Instructional Boundary Management. *Author created.*

overlapping area of school leadership should be conceptualized as one blended framework, which may be termed "instructional boundary management."

Figure 1 illustrates the suggested blended construct of instructional boundary management. The two ellipses represent the two frameworks of instructional leadership and boundary management. The arrows on the sides suggest that instructional leadership seeks to answer the questions of *what* and *why*, while boundary management seeks to answer the questions of *how* and *with whom*.

The two ellipses representing the two frameworks are located on both sides of the school boundary, involving both internal and external activities. Significantly, these two ellipses have a large area of overlap, which represents instructional boundary management. This overlap includes the activities of *instructional relating, instructional scouting, instructional persuading,* and *instructional empowering.*

From the paradoxical perspective, the overlapping area of instructional boundary management is a synthesis of instructional leadership and boundary management, where the two different frameworks are not mutually exclusive but rather complement each other. On the one hand, instructional boundary management can be seen as boundary management at the service of instructional leadership application, where principals seek to improve teaching and learning through boundary activities. Instructional leadership application thus provides the context for boundary management enacted by organizational actors through their social interactions.

At the same time, instructional boundary management can also be seen as instructional leadership application at the service of boundary management, where instructional leadership application enables the establishment and negotiation of school boundaries while helping determine relationships within the school and between the school and its environment, and while creating the levels of differentiation and integration necessary for effective functioning. Supporting each other in improving school academic performance and balancing the tension between internal and external demands, a paradoxical approach allows instructional leadership and boundary management to be combined to create the whole of instructional boundary management.

CONCLUSION

The goal of this chapter was to illustrate the paradoxical approach by pinpointing principals' behaviors that were found to simultaneously reflect instructional leadership application and boundary management. Therefore, this chapter utilized the paradoxical approach to present the instructional boundary management framework as a synthesis of instructional leadership application and boundary management.

This blended area of school leadership integrates a deep involvement in improving teaching and learning for all students together with monitoring of the school boundary's degree of permeability. Thus, these two different frameworks of instructional leadership and boundary management can be seen as merging with one another rather than competing for the principal's attention and limited time.

PRACTICAL RECOMMENDATIONS ON INSTRUCTIONAL BOUNDARY MANAGEMENT FOR POLICYMAKERS, PRINCIPAL EDUCATORS, SUPERINTENDENTS, AND PRINCIPALS

- Principals should engage in instructional leadership application and boundary management simultaneously through the boundary activity of *persuading*—distributing the instructional goals of the school both inside and outside the school.
- Principals should engage in instructional leadership application and boundary management simultaneously through the boundary activity of *empowering*—allowing teachers to move into instructional leadership roles, such as coaching other teachers and participating in planning committees.

- Principals should engage in instructional leadership application and boundary management simultaneously through the boundary activity of *scouting*—addressing teachers' teaching needs, helping teachers meet instructional challenges, and seeking external knowledge.
- Principals should engage in instructional leadership application and boundary management simultaneously through the boundary activity of *relating*—building trust and establishing healthy relationships both inside and outside the school with the aim of improving teaching and learning.

REFERENCES

Benoliel, P. (2017). Managing school management team boundaries and school improvement: An investigation of the school leader role. *International Journal of Leadership in Education, 20*(1), 57–86.

Benoliel, P., & Somech, A. (2018). A new perspective for understanding the role of school managers: The impact of principals' boundary activities on the effectiveness of school management team. *Teachers College Record, 120*(3), 1–40.

Druskat, V., & Wheeler, J. V. (2003). Managing from the boundary: The effective leadership of self-managing work teams. *Academy of Management Journal, 46*(4), 435–457.

Shaked, H., & Benoliel, P. (2020). Instructional boundary management: The complementarity of instructional leadership and boundary management. *Educational Management, Administration & Leadership, 48*(5), 821–839.

Urick, A. (2016). Examining US principal perception of multiple leadership styles used to practice shared instructional leadership. *Journal of Educational Administration, 54*(2), 152–172.

Valli, L., Stefanski, A., & Jacobson, R. (2018). School-community partnership models: Implications for leadership. *International Journal of Leadership in Education, 21*(1), 31–49.

Wang, F. (2018). Subversive leadership and power tactics. *Journal of Educational Administration, 56*(4), 398–413.

Epilogue
Answering the "So What?" Question

Complementing the existing research literature, this book provides novel data on principals' applications of instructional leadership. Specifically, insofar as instructional leadership is not applied in a vacuum, this book sheds light on the intricacy involved in educational leaders' application of instructional leadership within the complex system that is the school.

School leaders interact with multiple stakeholders, seeking to meet various goals and expectations, and their work is shaped by a wide range of contextual effects. Enhancing the application of instructional leadership is possible only if this complexity receives close attention. The current book offers some insights into how the application of instructional leadership is influenced by school goals, processes, relationships, and contexts.

One major complexity that is discussed at multiple points in this book pertains to the intricate system of interactions at play between instructional leadership application and principal-teacher relationships. On the one hand, the power of instructional leadership lies in the fact that it is task-oriented leadership, which focuses on what needs to be done to achieve preset goals, rather than relationship-oriented leadership, which focuses on how the principal and the teachers are connected.

In this sense, instructional leadership differs from transformational leadership. While under transformational leadership, principals concentrate on building trust and supporting teachers' needs; under instructional leadership principals concentrate on establishing clear goals and the efforts needed to achieve them. Thus, instructional leadership as an effective leadership approach may be seen as an authoritative approach involving supervision, evaluation, and monitoring, which do not attach primary importance to maintaining positive principal-teacher relationships. Put differently, instructional leadership is "a directive and top-down approach to school leadership" (Hallinger, 2003, p. 337).

On the other hand, insofar as school leadership is inherently based on relationships, the necessity of healthy relationships for instructional leadership application is undeniable. Principals as instructional leaders must be consummate relationship builders with diverse people and groups, especially with people different from themselves.

The central place that positive relationships occupy in instructional leadership application may explain why female principals consistently obtain higher ratings for applying instructional leadership than their male counterparts. Apparently, effective instructional leaders do not only focus on setting expectations and supervising teacher work, but also on cultivating interpersonal relationships.

Nevertheless, overly close principal-teacher relationships may serve as a major inhibiting factor of instructional leadership application. Such relationships might hinder many of the important elements inherent to instructional leadership, for example by preventing the principal from entering classrooms to observe, causing the principal to give inflated scores during teacher evaluations, making it difficult to dismiss bad teachers, and similar influences. Only a careful balance between all the considerations regarding the mutual effects between instructional leadership application and principal-teacher relationships will ensure a positive effect on student learning and academic results.

Another complexity of instructional leadership application discussed in this book deals with the question of the fundamental goal of schooling. Although identifying the primary task of educational institutions holds broad implications, to date there has been only minimal explicit discussion in the literature about the ultimate purpose toward which "good" education strives.

The instructional leadership approach emphasizes the academic goals of schooling, including expanding students' knowledge of essential subjects, developing their learning skills, and cultivating their curiosity. This premise of instructional leadership is consistent with current educational policy trends such as results-based accountability guidelines and comparative international studies. However, not all school principals agree with this outcome-focused instructional meta-goal for their school.

Some principals believe that the main objective of schooling should be non-academic—to meet students' emotional needs, impart moral values, and support their social integration. That is to say that the factors inhibiting instructional leadership application may stem not only from external constraints on principals and from their own skills but also from deep disagreements with some of the basic assumptions underlying instructional leadership.

One more area of complexity related to instructional leadership application as exemplified in this book involves the school context's influences on this leadership approach. Instructional leadership application is inseparable from the school context in which it is situated, and its frameworks should be adjusted to meet specific, local characteristics and needs.

Three prominent examples of how context may affect instructional leadership application are presented: how schools' family-like clan culture work environment can inhibit instructional leadership application, how low power distance as a characteristic of the national context can shape instructional leadership application, and how instructional leadership application can differ between rural and urban areas. These examples provide an answer to the question of whether context matters. The answer is clearly yes; context does matter.

Thus, unlike the previous path taken by a wide array of research that mostly ignored context, this book chooses a novel path showing that there is significant room for enhancing our understanding of how diverse geographical, cultural, and educational contexts influence the application of instructional leadership.

How can such complexities be addressed? All too often, instructional leaders are peddled simplistic solutions to complex situations. Unfortunately, as so many instructional leaders have discovered, these panaceas rarely work, because they are based on linear rather than systems thinking.

This book advocates for systems thinking as a possible enabler of instructional leaders' effective coping with real-life contemporary challenges in their schools, which often incorporate richly interconnected problem situations. We have elaborated comprehensively on the potential benefits of systems thinking in prior writings (see, for example, Shaked & Schechter, 2014, 2017).

Another major method suggested in this book is a paradoxical approach, which offers a "both/and" approach to conflicts. Instructional leaders are challenged by paradoxical situations all the time, facing contradictory yet interrelated demands and the resulting tensions. Therefore, they need to adopt a paradoxical lens, learning to create a synthesis, which occurs when competing expectations are met simultaneously.

Here my book—presenting new explorations on instructional leadership application—comes to an end. I hope that this book will be used by principal educators, policymakers, and especially school leaders themselves to meaningfully improve contemporary educational leadership and thereby today's schools.

REFERENCES

Hallinger, P. (2003). Leading educational change: Reflections on the practice of instructional and transformational leadership. *Cambridge Journal of Education*, *33*(3), 329–352.

Shaked, H., & Schechter, C. (2014). Systems school leadership: Exploring an emerging construct. *Journal of Educational Administration, 52*(6), 792–811.

Shaked, H., & Schechter, C. (2017). *Systems thinking for school leaders: Holistic leadership for excellence in education.* Springer.

Index

Arnold, R. D., 29
assistant principals: as advisors, 107, 110; authority avoidance of, 108–10; central instructional leadership behaviors avoidance of, 112; day-to-day operations involvement of, 105–6; as "forgotten leaders," xix, 81, 106, 112; influence sources access of, 106, 112; instructional leadership and, xix; instructional leadership boundaries of, 81; instructional leadership domains avoidance of, 105, 106; organizational hierarchy position of, 106; personnel management avoidance of, 110–11; practical recommendations for, 112–13; as principal personal and professional support, 106; strategic leadership avoidance of, 107–8; teacher monitoring and student achievement improvement duty of, 106, 112
authority avoidance, assistant principals and: "defiant" teacher handling in, 109–10; instructional decisions principal approval in, 110; instructional guidelines establishment and views of, 108–9

Barnes, K. E., 73
Benoliel, P., 127
big picture, xvi, 11, 30–31, 36, 107
Blase, Jo and Joseph, framework: instructional leadership key elements of, *xxxv–xxxvi*; professional growth promotion theme in, xxxiv; teacher reflection theme in, xxxiv
"both/and" orientation, 115, 117, 119–20
Brenninkmeyer, L. D., 28
Bulletin of the National Association of Secondary School Principals, xxx

Cameron, K. S., 56
Checkland, P., 29
Chicago school system, 84
clan culture, 43, 139; adhocracy culture in, 56; Cameron and Quinn organizational culture typology and, 56; "competing values framework" model in, 56; as family-like work environment, 55–56, 61; flexibility focus of, 56; freedom and autonomy use and, 57; as instructional leadership application inhibitor, xii, xviii, 43, 55; instructional leadership functions weakened by, 55, 57; instructional time protection in, 58–59, 61; as inward looking, 56;

141

market and hierarchy culture in, 56; practical recommendations on, 62; school intensity of, 57; supervision and evaluating instruction in, 57–58, 61; teacher incentives in, 60–61; "we-ness" sense in, 56
classroom observations, 57–58, 67, 110–11
community relationships, rural education and: equal authority in, 74; instructional leadership limit in, 73–74; opinion forcing and, 74; teacher work supervision and, 74–75
Content Knowledge, 3, 12; principals statements about, 6; recommendations on, 13; teacher subject matter in, 4
Cranston, N., 106
Curriculum Knowledge, 3; department heads and, 7, 12; principals statements about, 7–8; recommendations on, 13; school subjects and learning processes in, 4

Darling-Hammond, L., 95
day-to-day school operations, 46–47, 105–6
"defiant" teacher handling, 109–10
Descartes, René, 28
Druskat, V., 127

emotional well-being development, 49–50, 120–21
enablers, xviii; intrapersonal and interpersonal relationships examination in, 1; practical recommendations for, 13; principals professional knowledge base in, 1; principals' teaching and learning knowledge in, 4; Shulman seven knowledge categories research in, 6; Shulman's teachers' knowledge base typology of, 3–4; Spillane and Louis on Shulman's typology, 5; systems thinking in, 1

external boundary activities, instructional leadership and: academic priorities and parent expectations in, 132; curriculum and instruction information search in, 131; educational techniques and informal interactions in, 131–32; external instructional persuading in, 132; external instructional relating in, 131; external instructional scouting in, 131
external experts, 8–9
external stakeholder relationships, 23, 47, 107–8, 133; financial support seeking and statements about, 22; instructional leadership application and, 21–22; local municipal officials and statements about, 22; parents and principal statements about, 22; principals of other schools and statements about, 22

family-like work environment, 55–56, 60–61
feedback, 29, 39, 96
"forgotten leaders," xix, 81, 106, 112

General Pedagogical Knowledge, 3; classroom discipline problems addressing in, 7; classroom management and, 4; principals perceptions about, 6–7, 11; principals teaching methods proficiency in, 7; recommendations on, 13
Gilmour, A. F., 84
goal of schooling, instructional leadership application inhibitor, 138; future citizens preparation as, 50–51; mini-community view in, 50; non-academic and socializing task of, 49; personal responsibility and sense of mission in, 50; principals' perceptions about, 49; student achievements and, 50; student identity development as,

50; students' emotional well-being development as, 49–50
"good" teacher question, 98–99
Grissom, J. A., 46

Hallinger, P., xxxiii, *xxxv–xxxvi*, *xxxviii*, 66–67
Hallinger and Murphy framework: instructional leadership key elements of, *xxxv–xxxvi*; instructional program managing in, xxxiii; positive school learning climate development in, xxxiii; school mission defining in, xxxiii
Halverson, R., *xxxviii*, xxxix
holistic perspective, 28, 32–33, 39
Horng, E. L., 46
"How School Leadership Influences Student Learning" (Leithwood), xii

inhibitors, instructional leadership application: barriers in, 46; clan culture as, xii, xviii, 43, 55–62, 139; day-to-day school operations as, 46–47; educational systems as, xviii; goal of schooling as, 49–51, 138; main inhibitory perceptions to, 45; main perception-related factors in, 48; organizational norms and school stakeholders as, 47; practical recommendations for, 53; principal inadequate knowledge base in, 47; principal pressure and insufficient capabilities as, 47; principals avoidance of, 52–53; principals minimal time on, 45–46; principals' perceptions as, xviii, 43, 48; principal-teacher relationships as, 51–52; school leaders' roles as, 48–49; sufficient time lack in, 46; teacher territory encroachment and compliance in, 47
instructional boundary management, xix, 115; decentralization and bottom-up policy implementation in, 125–26;

Druskat and Wheeler's typology in, 127; external constituencies healthy relations maintenance for, 126; external persuading activities in, 128; external relating and scouting activities in, 127–28; instructional leadership and, 125; instructional leadership and external boundary activities in, 131–32; instructional leadership and internal boundary activities in, 128–31; internal and external activities in, 125; internal persuading and empowering activities in, 127; internal relating and scouting activities in, 127; paradoxical overlap in, 133–35; practical recommendations on, 135–36; principal behaviors in, 128; principals role juggling in, 126–27; principals transfer facilitation in, 126; schools multiple connections in, 126; tight and loose boundaries in, 126
instructional climate, xxix, xxxiii–xxxiv, *xxxvi*, xxxix, 66–68
instructional leadership. See *specific topics*
instructional program, xxix, xxxiii–xxxiv, *xxxv*, xxxix, 66–67
instructional time protection, clan culture and, 61; effective instructional leaders and, 58–59; principal leniency in, 59; teacher absenteeism in, 59; teacher instructional time use in, 59; teachers' family-work conflict in, 59
instructional vision, xxix, xxxiv, *xxxv*, xxxix, 66
internal boundary activities, instructional leadership and: dissemination activities and pedagogical vision in, 130; internal instructional empowering in, 130–31; internal instructional persuading in, 129–30; internal instructional

relating in, 128–29; internal instructional scouting in, 129; teacher instructional needs and, 129; teacher leaders and, 130–31; trust foundation in, 128–29
internal experts, 8–9
interpersonal relationships, teacher evaluation and: familiar consideration in, 88; good teacher relationships in, 88–89; principal statements about, 88–89
Israeli school system: contextual influences on, xvii; instructional leadership study in, xvii

Kelley, C., *xxxviii*, xxxix
Knowledge of Educational Contexts, 3, 5, 11–12; external influencing factors in, 4; principals external context use in, 10; principals local community and parent relationships in, 10; recommendations on, 13
Knowledge of Educational Ends, 3, 5, 12; goals and values in, 4; principals educational goals understanding in, 11; principals statements on, 11; recommendations on, 13
Knowledge of Learners and Their Characteristics, 3, 11; child development and group dynamics and academic heterogeneity familiarity and, 9; principals learner characteristics knowledge and student diversity in, 9–10; recommendations on, 13; student learning and, 4
Kraft, M. A., 84

leadership: concept and research on, xi; insightful perspectives on, xi–xiii; pedagogical content knowledge concept in, xi
Leadership Content Knowledge: internal and external experts for, 9; principals expectations in, 5–6; Stein and Nelson definition of, 5
leadership-for-learning framework, 64
Leithwood, Ken, xii, xxxvii, *xxxviii*, xxxix, 68
Lewis, M. W., 118
Louis, K. S., xxxvii, *xxxviii*, xxxix, 5, 68
low power distance, xviii, 43, 139; classroom observations in, 67; high power distance differences with, 65; instructional and transformational approaches and, 64; as instructional leadership application inhibitor, 63; instructional program management in, 67; instructional vision in, 66; leadership-for-learning framework and, 64; national context influence in, 63–64; organizational norms in, 66; organizational redesign in, 68; policy borrowing in, 64–65, 69; positive school learning climate in, 67–68; practical recommendations on, 69–70; respect earning in, 65; school mission challenges in, 66–67; school's mission collaborative development in, 66; as sociocultural norm, 63; superintendents' instructional leadership demands and, 68–69; teacher development in, 68; transformational leadership and, 64; workplace informality in, 65–66

Marks, H. M., xxxi–xxxii
May, H., 46
mid-level school leaders, 23; informal relationships with, 20; principals distributed instructional leadership to, 17; principal support of and statements about, 19; secret partners and principal statements about, 19–20
multidimensional view adoption, 30, 36–37, 118–19
Murphy, J., xxxiii, *xxxv–xxxvi*, *xxxviii*, 47, 66–67

Nelson, B. S., 5
neoliberalism, 94
non-academic school goals, paradoxical approach and, 49; as primary task in, 120; principals views on, 121, 138; student emotional well-being and achievement in, 120–21

organizational norms, 47, 66

paradoxical approach, instructional leadership application and, xii, xix, 139; "both/and" orientation in, 115, 117; conflicting perspectives in, 118–19; contradiction handling in, 122–23; decision delay in, 117, 119; "either/or" challenges contrast with, 117–18; as flexible and resilient, 118; multidimensional view adoption and, 118–19; non-academic school goals and, 120–21; non-paradoxical and paradoxical leaders in, 118; people management and, 118; practical recommendations for, 123; principal role beliefs in, 119–20; principal-teacher relationships in, 121–22; relevance of, 123; Smith and Lewis definition of, 118; systems thinking relation in, 118
paradoxical overlap, instructional boundary management and: framework complement in, 134; instructional boundary management construct in, 133–34, *134*; instructional leaders focus in, 133; instructional leadership application and boundary management service in, 134–35; instructional mission and external stakeholders in, 133; question addressing in, 133; two frameworks in, 133
parents: academic priorities and expectations of, 132; principal relationships with, 10, 22; rural education and, 73, 75–77

parents and community characteristics, rural education and: academic achievements unimportance in, 75; principals' own supervisors and, 76; school community expectations in, 76
patterns identification, 38
Pedagogical Content Knowledge, xi, 3, 12; internal or external expertise agents for, 8; particular subject and, 4; principals statements about, 8–9; recommendations on, 13; Shulman on, 4–5
performance data interpretation, systems thinking and, 40; data use in, 37; factor monitoring for, 38; feedback delay in, 39; holistic perspective in, 39; major patterns identification in, 38; multidimensional view adoption for, 37; reductionist thinking and, 37–38; student achievement pressure in, 37; temporal issues in, 38–39; time delay awareness lack in, 39
personnel management avoidance, assistant principals and: as advisors, 110; classroom observations in, 110–11; human resources as principal management, 110; inservice teacher evaluation and, 111; performance evaluations and, 110; resume screening and interviewing participation of, 110; teacher dismissal in, 111
policy borrowing, 64–65, 69
Preston, J. P., 73
principal role beliefs, paradoxical approach and: "both/and" proposition in, 119–20; conflicting commitments juggling in, 119; teaching and learning involvement and, 120
principals. *See specific topics*
principal-teacher relationships, 23, 72; good relationship characteristics and principal statements about, 20; group and individual, 21; instructional

leadership application and, 16, 20; new instructional initiatives opposition and, 20–21; openness in, 21; teacher method discourse in, 21; transformational leadership and, 16, 17, 51–52

principal-teacher relationships, instructional leadership application inhibitor, 138; damage perception in, 51; instructional leadership application limit in, 52; instructional supervision impingement and, 51; transformational leadership approach and, 51–52; work relationship perception in, 52

principal-teacher relationships, paradoxical approach and: principals statements about, 122; teacher supervision in, 121

Printy, S. M., xxxi–xxxii

professional learning communities, systems thinking and, 32, 40; collaborative atmosphere promotion for, 34; collective wisdom in, 35; conceptual basis for, 34; instructional leadership application enabling in, 36–37; multidimensional view adoption in, 36; other opinions consideration in, 36; principals on, 34–35; teachers as part of whole in, 34–35

Quinn, R. E., 56

reductionist thinking, 28, 37–38

relationships, instructional leadership application and, 23; as decentralized, 16; external stakeholder relationships in, 21–22; functional responsibilities sharing in, 17; good relationship building capacity for, 16; mid-level school leaders and, 17, 19–20; practical recommendations for, 24; principal-teacher relationships in, 16, 20–21; relationship cultivation in, 15; relationship-oriented functions for, 16; relationships types in, 17; self-awareness and principal statements about, 18; self-discipline and principal statements about, 19; self-regulation and principal statements about, 18–19; specific goal setting and monitoring in, 16–17; task-oriented leadership in, 16, 137; teachers' teaching strategies influence in, 15; transformational leadership and, 16, 17

Richmond, B., 29

Robinson, V. M. J., xxxi, xxxii, xxxvii, *xxxviii*, 27–28, 96

Rothman, R., 84

rural education, 99, 139; children in, 72; community relationships in, 73–75; contextual factors in, 71–72, 76; informal meetings for, 72–73; instructional leadership application in, xviii, 43; as instructional leadership application inhibitor, 71, 73; parent and community communication in, 73, 76–77; parents and community characteristics in, 75–76; people-centered leadership in, 73; practical recommendations on, 77; principal-teacher relationships in, 72; principal visibility in, 73; relational leadership style in, 72; school primary task in, 76; teaching staff recruitment in, 72

school curriculum, systems thinking and, 40; big picture grasping in, 30–31; coordination as major issue and ongoing process in, 31–32; curriculum and instruction and assessment coordination in, 31; curriculum as spiral in, 33; holistic development of, 32–33; interrelations among, 34; parts interaction in, 31; principal view on, 32; professional peer learning community

Index

development in, 32; reading comprehension development and, 33
school leaders: close relationships and, xii; instructional boundary management and, xix; instructional leadership application and research on, xv–xvi, xix; instructional leadership as DNA of, xii; instructional leadership principal's perspective in, xvii; instruction and curriculum improvement involvement of, xv; interview research on, xvii; journal articles on, xviii; paradoxical approach and, xii, xix; as relationship based, 15; study participants confidentiality of, xvii–xviii
school leadership frameworks, 39–40; "accountability" movement in, xxix; Blase, Jo and Joseph, two themes in, xxxiv; as context-dependent, 71; definition of, xxix; "effective schools" and, xxx; ethical and social considerations in, xxxii; four key elements in, *xxxviii*; Hallinger and Murphy framework as, xxxiii, xxxvii, *xxxviii*; Halverson and Kelley five domain model of, *xxxviii*, xxxix; high-quality teaching and students' academic results in, xxxi; "instructional" leadership and "transformational" leadership difference in, xxxi–xxxii; instructional leadership key elements in, *xxxv–xxxvi*, xxxvii; Leithwood and Louis four core practices in, xxxvii, *xxxviii*, xxxix; Marks and Printy on, xxxi–xxxii; past principal duties in, xxx; principals and student influence in, xxix–xxxi; principals expectations and top priority in, xxix–xxx, xxxii–xxxiii; research literature on, xxx, xxxii; resource acquisition and social advocacy in, xxxvii; Robinson on leadership elements in, xxxi, xxxvii, *xxxviii*; school middle leaders duties in, xxxi; Stronge five essential features of, xxxiv; Weber five dimensions in, xxxiii
school leaders' roles, instructional leadership application inhibitor: as extra-school world bridge, 48; facilitation task of, 49; principal role definition view in, 48; as resources and budget manager, 48; as teacher enabling, 48; teaching and learning ineffectual involvement and, 49
school mission, 107, 133; Hallinger and Murphy framework defining of, xxxiii; low power distance and, 66–67
schools: as complex organization, xvi, xix; instructional leadership and, xvi, xviii; nonlinear relationships understanding in, xvi; teacher evaluation in, xviii
Senge, P., 28–29
Shaked, Haim, xi
Shulman, Lee, xi, 3–6
Smith, W. K., 118
Spillane, J. P., 5, 28
Stein, M. K., 5
strategic leadership avoidance, assistant principals and: as advisors, 107; external stakeholder view of, 107–8; instructional discussions and, 108; instructional improvement limit of, 107; school's instructional mission in, 107
Stronge, J. H., xxxiv, *xxxv–xxxvi*
student achievement, 37, 50, 106, 112
supervision and evaluating instruction, clan culture and, 61; classroom observations and, 57–58; national achievement tests low performance in, 58; principals student compromise in, 58; teaching quality in, 58
Supovitz, J. A., 46

systems thinking, xviii, 1, 118, 139; Arnold and Wade opinion of, 29; big picture seeing in, 30; complex problem-solving in, 27; concept of, 28; feedback loops and, 29; holistic perspective in, 28; indirect influencing in, 30; as instructional leadership application enabler, 28; instructional leadership areas of, 27; main complementary meanings of, 29; multidimensional view adoption for, 30; performance data interpretation in, 37–39; practical recommendations for, 40; professional learning communities in, 34–37; real-life situations facing in, 28; reductionist approach contrast with, 28; Richmond and Checkland on, 29; Robinson's model of, 27–28; school curriculum and, 30–34; school leaders application of, 30; as school leadership approach, 39–40; Senge definition of, 28–29; significance evaluating in, 30; as study of wholes, 27

teacher development, xxix, xxxiv, *xxxvi*, xxxix, 66

teacher dismissal unpleasantness, principals and: as difficult and painful task, 100–101; ineffective teacher research and, 100; long-term relationships in, 101; major difficulties in, 100; national unionized teacher tenure policies barrier in, 100; rejection of, 101–2; teacher economic damage and, 101; tenure and interpersonal connection in, 101

teacher evaluation, 111; Chicago school system ratings and, 84; as instructional leadership useless component, 81; interpersonal relationships in, 88–89; over-evaluation in, 84–85; practical recommendations on, 90; principals high rating of, 84; rating research in, 84; school principals considerations in, 83, 85, 89–90; teacher evaluation measurements imprecision in, 87–88; teaching improvement ineffectiveness in, 86–87; time constraints and prioritization in, 85–86; two basic purposes of, 83–84; "Widget Effect" in, 84

teacher evaluation measurements, teacher evaluations and: inaccurate measurement in, 87; principals statements about, 87–88; qualifications and assets view in, 87; specific educational context in, 88

teacher incentives, clan culture and: event arrangements in, 61; family atmosphere undermining in, 60; non-compliance with deadlines response in, 60; positive relationship maintenance in, 60; teaching quality and student success in, 60

teacher job suitability, principals and: fit conceptual frameworks in, 94; hiring and firing practices utilization in, 95; human resources tasks avoidance of, 96, 102; human resources tasks view of, 93, 95; inherited or learned ability question in, 94–95; as instructional leadership essential component, 93–94; instruction feedback and, 96; neoliberalism and, 94; personality characteristics possession in, 95; practical recommendations on, 103; "right" attributes for, 94; supervision-evaluation component of, 96; teacher dismissal unpleasantness in, 100–102; teachers as commodities, 94; teacher selection uncertainty in, 97–100; teaching ability development in, 95; two areas of complexity in, 96; uncertainty and apprehension in, 102

teacher leaders, xxxiv, 12, 130–31

teacher selection uncertainty, principals and: clarity and knowledge lack in, 97; complexity of, 97; customary interview procedure efficiency and, 97; "good" teacher question in, 98; hiring process's limited validity explanations for, 97; instinct and gut feelings or intuition use in, 99–100; no systematic training for, 98, 99; rural areas and, 99; specific educational context for, 99; teacher effectiveness multidimensionality in, 98–99

teaching improvement, teacher evaluation and: ineffectiveness of, 86; instruction quality in, 87; principals statements about, 86–87; tenure policy and, 86–87

tenure policy, 86–87, 100–101

time constraints and prioritization, teacher evaluation and: ineffectiveness or uselessness perception in, 85; as multi-step process, 85; principals statements about, 85–86

Toch, T., 84

transformational leadership: instructional leadership differences with, xxxi–xxxii, 137; low power distance in, 64; principal-teacher relationships in, 16, 17, 51–52

Wade, J. P., 29
Weber, J., xxxiii, *xxxv–xxxvi*
Weisberg, D., 84
Wheeler, J. V., 127
"Widget Effect," 84

About the Author

Prof. Haim Shaked is the President of Hemdat College of Education, Sdot Negev, Israel. As a scholar-practitioner with almost twenty years of experience as a school principal, his research focuses on principalship, and in particular on instructional leadership and system thinking in school leadership. As a skilled qualitative research methodologist, his empirical studies are well-crafted and tend to include a large number of interviews and focus groups. He has published more than fifty refereed research articles, book chapters, edited books, and authored books. His book (co-author Chen Schechter, foreword by Michael Fullan) *Systems Thinking for School Leaders: Holistic Leadership for Excellence in Education* was published by Springer Press. His book *Leading Holistically: How Schools, Districts, and States Improve Systemically* (co-editors Chen Schechter & Alan J. Daly, foreword by Michael Fullan) was published by Routledge. His book *Preparing Future Leaders for Social Justice: Bridging Theory and Practice through a Transformative Andragogy,* 2nd Edition (co-author Kathleen M. Brown) was published by Rowman & Littlefield.

www.ingramcontent.com/pod-product-compliance
Lightning Source LLC
Chambersburg PA
CBHW020125240426
43673CB00038B/592